GW00372120

THE
SCIENCE & THEATRE
OF
≈COFFEE≈

{ ROAST - GRIND - BREW - SERVE }

SOUTH WEST INDEPENDENT COFFEE GUIDE

the INSIDER'S GUIDE TO THE BEST INDY COFFEE VENUES AND ROASTERS

★ ★ ★ ★ ★ ★ ★ ★ ★ ★

№2

Salt Media, 5 Cross Street, Devon, EX31 1BA.
www.saltmedia.co.uk
Tel: 01271 859299
Email: ideas@saltmedia.co.uk

Salt Media Indy Coffee Guide team:
Jo Rees, Nick Cooper, Catherine Jones,
Chris Sheppard, Tamsin Powell,
Gemma Chilton, Kathryn Lewis,
Marcus Chapman
Design: Salt Media
Illustrations: Dale Stiling

**A big thank you to the *Indy Coffee Guide*
committee, the headline sponsors** Schluter
and Yeo Valley, **and sponsors** Beyond the
Bean, Bunn, Clifton Coffee Roasters,
Extract Coffee Roasters, Origin Coffee,
Sanremo UK and Ireland.

Coffee shops, cafes and roasters are
invited to be included in the guide based on
meeting criteria set by our committee. This
includes a high quality coffee experience for
visitors, use of UK roasted beans and being
independently run.

www.indycoffee.guide

THE EXPLODING BAKERY

MAP.№34 | PAGE.№78

BRAZIER COFFEE ROASTERS
MAP.№100 | PAGE.№120

FOREWORD

A year ago, when we published the first *South West Independent Coffee Guide* it was a thrilling moment, marking the culmination of huge amounts of planning, discussion, meetings, interviews, writing and designing by a team of like-minded, coffee loving, people. Twelve months down the line we're so proud to publish the second South West edition, to go with the Northern guide which came out in early summer 2015, and the Scottish guide which launches at the start of 2016.

'ADVENTUROUS. DEDICATED. GENUINE. GENEROUS. THERE'S SOMETHING ABOUT SPECIALITY COFFEE PEOPLE ...'

Along with updates on many familiar names from last year, there's a raft of new venues and roasters to tell you about in this year's guide, which goes to show – if you needed persuading - that the growth of the speciality coffee scene in the South West shows no signs of abating.

Adventurous. Dedicated. Genuine. Generous. From importers to roasters, trainers and baristas, there's something about speciality coffee people... maybe it's simply that single-minded passion and willingness to share their love of coffee. Whatever it is, let's raise a coffee cup to them all.

Catherine Jones
Editor

🐦 @indycoffeeguide

CONTENTS

CLEVER DRIPPER

'THE FOLLOW-UP ALBUM IS ALWAYS A TRICKY ONE'

ANDREW TUCKER
CLIFTON COFFEE ROASTERS

WELCOME

'WE'RE BACK WITH ISSUE TWO OF THE INDY COFFEE GUIDE, AND THE REVOLUTION GOES FROM STRENGTH TO STRENGTH,' SAYS ANDREW TUCKER OF CLIFTON COFFEE ROASTERS

Last year's *Indy Coffee Guide* was the first physical representation of just how far the speciality coffee industry has come in the South West.

Until five years ago, you could count the number of coffee roasters in the South West on one hand. Today we find ourselves among a plethora of some of the country's finest roasters – and I'm proud to be among them.

their businesses on quality first and foremost.

While we all have slightly different approaches to roasting or brewing coffee, we're all committed to ensuring our customers get to drink a better cup of coffee.

The committee behind the *South West Independent Coffee Guide* makes no secret of its aim, which is to guide coffee

'TO GUIDE COFFEE DRINKERS OUT OF THE BIG CORPORATE CHAINS AND INTO THE INDEPENDENT SPECIALITY STORES'

Of course, the follow-up album is always a tricky one, but the great feedback we received about the first edition of the guide has given us the confidence to produce something bigger and better this year, while maintaining its integrity.

Many coffee shop owners report new customers having found them through the guide and a growing abundance of brilliant independent coffee shops are doing an amazing job of introducing the public to speciality coffee.

The roasters play a key part too, of course, with new ones springing up in the South West all the time. Along with more established roasting businesses in the region, they represent our united commitment to coffee quality and the fact that more cafe owners are basing

drinkers out of the big corporate chains and into the independent speciality stores which support our local economy and help move this wonderful industry forward.

It's an exciting time to be roasting, serving and drinking coffee, and the South West has huge potential for speciality coffee to become mainstream. If our guide plays its part in that process we have something to be very proud of.

Andrew Tucker

Head of Coffee at Clifton Coffee Roasters and *South West Independent Coffee Guide* committee member

BLASTING
INTO THE FUTURE

PLAYGROUND COFFEE HOUSE
MAP.№22 | PAGE.№63

THERE'SE NO LET UP IN THE SPEED AT WHICH TRENDS IN SPECIALITY COFFEE ARE DEVELOPING. SO WHAT'S COMING OVER THE HORIZON? WE ASKED SOME INDUSTRY EXPERTS

MEAN MACHINES

'There's going to be an increasing pursuit of accuracy and consistency in everything – from grinder dosing and performance through to coffee machine extraction management', says Andrew Tucker of Sanremo UK. *'At the same time, the ability of the specialist to manipulate the coffee flavours through the extraction will increase.'*

Andrew Tucker from Clifton Coffee adds, *'the past 12 months have seen an explosion in the number of people switching to temperature regulated, grind-on-demand espresso grinders. Combined with gravimetric dosing of espresso machines over traditional volumetrics, this will continue to push brewing standards further.'*

INVASION

Is a US super brand set to arrive in the UK? The arrival of one of the American big four (Stumptown, Intelligentsia, Counter Culture and Blue Bottle) could change the landscape big time, thinks Clifton's Andrew. *'Blue Bottle successfully launched in Japan with a roastery and two coffees last year, and there's a rumour of a London launch in the near future.'*

These major players, with their hefty financial backers and ability to wholesale and retail directly-traded speciality coffees is a model now being pursued by many UK roasters. *'But,'* he asks, *'who will be the first to successfully cross the Atlantic?'*

'ON THE COCKTAIL HIT LIST WHEN COMBINED WITH ALCOHOL, SIGNATURE DRINKS ARE GOING DOWN A STORM'

FILTER FANS

'Expect to see a lot more bulk brew filter coffee equipment making its way on to bars up and down the country,' says Clifton's Andrew. That's because, *'demand for filter is higher than brew bars can cope with,'* says Ed Gooding of Bunn, which is why he thinks machinery's improving. *'The multiples are now looking at filter coffee as more than just a cheaper option. It's a trend driven by the speciality shops.'*

COLD BREW

'There's been a lot of noise around cold brew coffee,' according to Clifton's Andrew, *'in particular, nitrogen-infused cold brew, which increases shelf life, helps keep the flavour and gives it a creamier texture.*

'But despite a lot of talk, the UK market is still very much in its infancy as far as cold brew coffee is concerned,' he says. *'A cold climate doesn't help, as most people still prefer their coffee hot, but it's only a matter of time before it's recognised as an alternative to mainstream soft drinks. It can be truly delicious if brewed correctly.'*

SIGNATURE AND SEASONAL

Signature drinks, once just served within the realm of barista championships, could be making more of an impact on the streets. Seasonal, creative and on the cocktail list when combined with alcohol, signature drinks are going down a storm at Origin's Shoreditch store. *'They're a way to celebrate the strengths of the coffee and develop and show it in a different way,'* says head of wholesale, Dan Fellows (who came fourth in the 2015 UK Barista Championships). *'It gives people the chance to be creative and individual.'*

ONE
FOR THE ROAD

BIKES AND BREWS GO HAND IN HAND, SO WE SENT CYCLING
GEEK MARCUS CHAPMAN AND CRANKHOUSE COFFEE'S
DAVE STANTON TO TRY OUT THE LATEST IN "ANYTIME,
ANYWHERE" COFFEE – THE CAFFLANO

It's hard to ignore the cycle explosion that's happening across the UK right now. With over three million bikes sold in 2014, it seems the country has gone cycle crazy.

And there's one common bond that all cyclists seem to share: an all consuming passion for good coffee. Yep, cycling and coffee go together like fish and chips.

Across the country, cyclists plan their entire ride around their next caffeine fix, both for the taste and the reported performance benefits the "black doctor" brings. Forget EPO, the number one cycling drug is caffeine, so much so that up until 2004 the World Anti-Doping Agency set a limit of eight shots of espresso per day for competing cyclists.

Cycling's link with caffeine has a rich history, especially through the professional peloton. In the 1960s the Italian espresso machine manufacturer Faema sponsored a pro team, which included the legendary Eddy Merckx, to promote its innovative machine. Nowadays, Chris Hoy famously travels everywhere with his own rather large espresso machine.

BECOME A BARISTA

So what happens if you are out in the wild, with legs like stringy spaghetti from grinding the pedals all day, with not even a lowly service station on the horizon to fuel your tired engine?

The Cafflano, with it's "anytime, anywhere" boast, is throwing its barista hat into the ring to solve this very problem. Complete with grinder, metal filter dripper, drip kettle and tumbler, all neatly slotted together - the Cafflano is a super portable, all-in-one coffee maker.

'FORGET EPO, THE NUMBER ONE
CYCLING DRUG IS CAFFEINE'

THE MISSION

I called in Dave Stanton from Exeter's Crankhouse Coffee to help put it to the test. Dave is a self confessed cycle geek and one of the finest new breed of coffee roasters in the South West. With a tent, a bag of beans, the trusty Trangia and a few supplies, we stuffed the Cafflano deep in our panniers and hit the north Devon coast.

FRESH AS A DAISY

Out on the road, there was a certain romance in brewing our own coffee with the Cafflano, and the satisfaction in knowing it was the freshest it could be. It certainly helped that Dave had brought along a bag of his just roasted beans. Not only were we provided with the highest quality caffeine hit for our tired legs, but there was also a certain campfire smugness in having rustled it up in the wild. Far better than a £3 coffee that blisters the roof of your mouth and tastes like a stagnant pond.

Dave says, *'Pre-ground coffee seeps flavour from the moment it's ground, as exposure to the air starts to degrade the potential flavour of the carefully grown, harvested, processed and roasted beans. Grind only what you need and brew immediately to get the absolute best flavour – which is where the Cafflano earns its stripes.'*

DRINK COFFEE
Ride faster

Recent tests by Glasgow University concluded that one strong cup of coffee boosted performance and aided concentration.

Cyclists in the test who got 0.7mg of caffeine per kilo of body weight rode significantly longer than cyclists with no caffeine.

So if you know your body weight, just multiply it roughly by 0.7 to see how much caffeine is going to add zip to your legs.

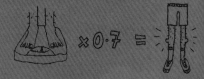

Knowing the caffeine dose is crucial, as espresso can contain anything between 50mg and 300mg, while the Department of Health reckons a standard mug of filter coffee has 140g of caffeine.

It's a fact: drink coffee, ride faster!

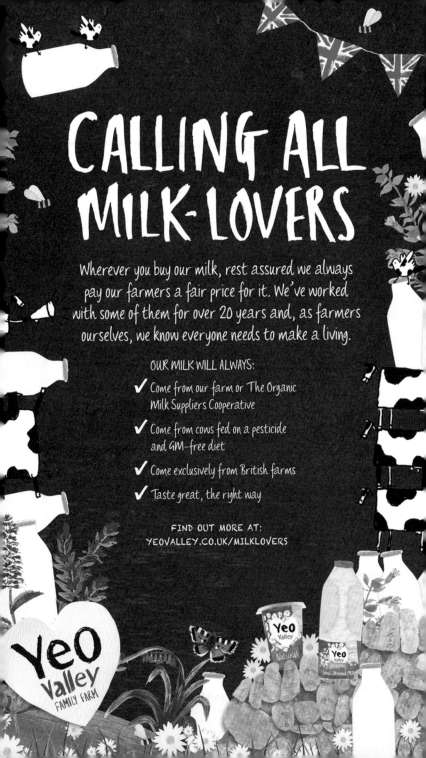

IN PURSUIT *of perfection*

UK BARISTA CHAMP, MAXWELL COLONNA-DASHWOOD, TALKS ABOUT CHASING MICRONS IN THE BREWING FAST LANE

On one level, the preparation of a cup of coffee is a simple procedure. A roasted and ground seed is mixed with hot water, some of the ground seed dissolves into the water, and voilà, we have a beverage also known as a cup of coffee.

On the other hand, this seemingly simple process is filled with layers of complexity. How much of the ground seed do we extract? Which compounds do we get and which do we want? It turns out this little seed is complex, and subtle changes in the extraction process will result in dramatic flavour differences.

Speciality coffee is all about this precious flavour. It's about capturing and consistently recreating the best aspects of a very special, carefully grown and roasted seed.

GEAR SHIFT

The extent of the machinery and equipment we use to make a cup of coffee reflects its complexity. And as we value coffee more and more and we learn new intricacies, the equipment we use needs to evolve to meet these demands, and help push coffee forwards.

Some developments with equipment represent small marginal gains, but in speciality coffee marginal gains matter. It's like the precision of a Formula One car; an improvement may gain the driver half a second, but this seemingly small improvement has a big impact.

The rate at which speciality coffee is growing and developing means that some of the changes in equipment go way beyond this and represent shifts in preparation, for example, the emergence of scales that are built into drip trays.

DAILY GRIND

The depths of the grinding world have arguably only been lightly mined. A decade ago it was a big change to move over to attaching a timer to a grinder and attempting to grind only the amount of coffee needed for each drink. But to actually do this, with no waste and to achieve the specific weight of ground coffee required, represents the next race among equipment manufacturers.

Recreating your recipe (a weight of coffee to a weight of water) is the central goal of the machine grinder combo, but there are other hidden variables. How even is the grind? How consistent is the water temperature and the flow rate of water from the group head?

'IT'S LIKE FORMULA ONE; AN IMPROVEMENT MAY GAIN THE DRIVER HALF A SECOND, BUT IT HAS A BIG IMPACT'

CHASING MICRONS

I did a show where I made coffee for a company that builds manufacturing machines for a Formula One team. The people I met had a saying: 'we're chasing microns' – a tiny unit of measurement. The best machines on the market could cut a material to a staggering 0.3 of a micron. I don't know what slogan we could use in coffee, but the passion to achieve perfection is very much the same.

SCHOOL OF MILK

GETTING THE MILK RIGHT IS ALMOST AS MUCH OF AN ART AS MAKING THE COFFEE ITSELF. ALEX PASSMORE OF CORNWALL'S ORIGIN COFFEE GIVES A MASTERCLASS

'The hardest thing with getting milk right is its quality and consistency,' says Alex Passmore, national training manager for Origin. *'Although,'* he adds, *'some things are not in our control, like the holding temperature of milk from dairy to us.'* (Somewhere between one and three degrees centigrade, he says).

SO, TEMPERATURE'S IMPORTANT THEN?

Alex says when you're steaming milk for espresso, the maximum temperature should be about 65°c. *'Milk at this temperature is at its maximum perceived sweetness – before and after that it drops. It's how our tongues perceive it. Warm milk is a lot more palatable and tastes a lot sweeter,'* he says.

THEN THERE'S THE SCIENCE BIT ...

The proteins in milk have two parts, one of which doesn't like water (the hydrophobic bit). They're all tangled up in chains but these chains get broken through agitation or heat. When that happens the hydrophobic part gets exposed and grabs on to the first thing it finds that's not water – in steaming milk, it's air. Our little proteins bind to the air, trap it and, hey presto! - a bubble is made.

The protein coated air bubbles stick together but, because milk is denser than foam, after some time it separates and the bubbles burst. The small bubbles in a good microfoam slow this down and, because full fat milk is thicker, it will also drain more slowly. The fat of course is also important, Alex says, because it adds to the "mouthfeel" of the coffee. *'That silky, buttery mouthfeel is the fat in milk. It also holds the bubbles in place for longer,'* he says.

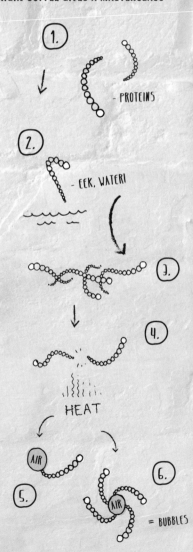

1.

– PROTEINS

2.

– EEK, WATER!

3.

4.

HEAT

5. AIR

6. AIR

= BUBBLES

MICROFOAM PERFECTION

Put air in the milk as early in the heating process as possible, because as soon as it reaches 30°c it's not as receptive to being stressed. Put the air in slowly, with the steam tip just below the surface, to make sure the bubbles are small. As soon as it reaches hand temperature (30°c), stop putting air in, as you'll only end up with bigger bubbles.

Texturing is done throughout the steaming. This breaks down the bigger bubbles and makes the surface smoother. Texturing is not adding air but moving it around, swirling it in the milk jug with the wand as high up in the body of the milk as possible. There's no reason to go to the bottom of the milk jug at all.

HOW MUCH MILK?

Flat white: no bigger than a 6oz cup and no more than a ¼cm foam – a thin layer. Always a double shot of espresso.

Latte: ½cm foam, but in a larger 7-12 oz cup. Either one or two shots of espresso.

Cappuccino: *'Following the Speciality Coffee Association of Europe (SCAE) guidelines, it's 1cm to 1½ cm foam. It must have lots of rich microfoam,'* says Alex, *'and it'll feel more concentrated because there's more air in the cup and less coffee mixing with the milk.'*

'Overall, you need to make coffee accessible,' says Alex. *'People will all have different tastes but what matters is that baristas are trained.'*

'THAT SILKY, BUTTERY MOUTHFEEL IS THE FAT – AND IT HOLDS THE BUBBLES IN PLACE FOR LONGER'

ALEX'S MILKY DOS AND DON'TS

MILK SHOULD BE AS COLD AS POSSIBLE – HOLDING TEMPERATURE IS 3-5°C

DON'T RE-HEAT OR RE-STEAM THE SAME MILK. IT DOESN'T HOLD ITS FOAM THE SAME AFTERWARDS

USE CLEAN, RINSED AND COLD MILK JUGS

DON'T OVERTHINK IT TOO MUCH WHEN STEAMING MILK. IT'S SIMPLE REALLY, JUST ADDING AIR AND TEXTURING!

SHOULD WE EVEN BE USING MILK?

'I approach milky drinks tentatively as they are quite filling,' says Alex. 'I look at them as being like the dessert part of a meal. At Origin we have smaller milk-based coffees, and we use a high quality milk. It all depends on how delicate the coffee is – some Kenyan based espressos, for example, are so delicate, they don't cut through the milk.'

GREAT EFFORT

SCHLUTER

Speciality African Coffees from Schluter
— Since 1858 —

For all your African coffee needs

We stock a full range of speciality coffee from the continent of Africa in store in the UK. We can deliver quantities from single pallets upwards to any destination in the UK, Europe or across the world.

Malawi

Ethiopia

Tanzania

Rwanda

Burundi

Kenya

Cameroon

DRC

Uganda

T: +44 (0)151 498 6500 | E: liverpool@schluter.ch | www.schlutercoffee.co.uk

SCHLUTER
the joy of african coffee

AFRICAN ADVENTURES

PIGS ON BIKES, SLAUGHTERED GOATS AND CABS WITH NO HEADLIGHTS – IT'S ALL IN A DAY'S WORK FOR THE INTREPID EXPLORERS SOURCING BEANS IN AFRICA

GOING LOCAL IN THE RIFT VALLEY

Bean importer Phil Schluter has travelled many times to East Africa, the land where he spent much of his childhood. There's a history of adventuring in his family - indeed, his coffee growing grandmother would recount the time she was lowered down the Rift Valley in a basket and also the occasion she saw a hippo bite a boat in half on Lake Baringo. So it's no surprise to learn that Phil's at home in the depths of the African countryside. *'It's a privilege to see places in the world that no one ever sees,'* he says, before recalling one memorable trip to source organic beans in the Gololcha region of Western Harrar in Ethiopia.

After a hassle with the Hilton Hotel in the capital Addis Ababa (the hotel had given his rooms away because, despite being transported by its own shuttle bus, Phil's group had apparently got there too late), they set off for the small town of Nazret. *'Only after I'd paid for our return room and begged them to keep it for us,'* he says.

At Nazret he found himself waking at 5am in a run-down hotel to find two monkeys going through his colleague's luggage – he had left the door open for air. 'Big mistake.'

The day's trip began with a drive to a point 3,000m up, overlooking the Rift Valley. 'We were on an escarpment, and could see the rolling green hills for miles and miles. It was absolutely beautiful.'

Making their way through a V-shaped crack between rocks, they followed a very bad road (which became a river when it rained), then dropped almost vertically, 1km in altitude, into the bottom of the valley, before driving for two hours across and into virgin rain forest.

'We met with the locals who shook our hands, then went and slaughtered a goat which we ate with them.' After handing out footballs to the children, Phil shared a bottle of coke with the local imam, before they continued on their way.

On the return journey, the car broke down and they found themselves at 9pm on a rough road miles from anywhere. A passing bus took them back to Nazret, but they needed to get to the capital, Addis Ababa. 'Our hosts said not to get a taxi', but after a futile wait for another bus they hailed a cab and set off – in a vehicle which had no headlights and a door that didn't close. 'It only went at 40mph and it took 10 seconds from turning the wheel for the car to change direction.' It took them more than four hours to reach Addis at 2am. And guess what? 'They'd only gone and given our rooms away again,' sighs Phil.

PANDEMONIUM AND PANCAKES

Bertie Sewell was working for an advertising agency in the centre of London, before he decided, rather bravely, to pack it in and head off on his own to Southern Tanzania, for a job overseeing a coffee warehouse.

On arrival he found everything broken. *'It was pandemonium at first,'* he admits, and then there was the hotel dinner experience. *'I went to this tiny little hotel. The menu had at least 12-15 items on it, but every time I asked for something, they didn't have it.'* At a loss, and being the only person in the dining room, he finally asked what they did have. *'A chicken'* was the reply. A chicken was quite literally what they had - and only after buying one off a neighbour and slaughtering it.

Bertie had to learn fast about life in east Africa, and get used to the unexpected. On one occasion he was based in a small town called Mbinga where, as an operations manager,

he worked with around 15 remote washing stations. *'You'd get to them by really winding roads, or no roads at all. They'd start harvesting in the afternoon and it would take a long time to get back to the station to process it. Often if something broke at a factory, I'd get a panicky call and then I'd be bombing off in a bus in the middle of the night to try and sort broken machines.'*

On his own in a strange country, miles away from home, he admits, *'there were times when I'd feel a bit downtrodden. But every day I'd wake up and see something spectacular – like the view. There's no power for miles around, so you wake up with the sun at dawn, go get your cup of chai and pancakes, and you're up and running.'*

'I'd then meet the team before we set off for the bank in a Land Rover with a load of coffee sacks - because everything's done in cash.' Sacks? *'You need them because you have to withdraw lots of cash - one dollar is around 2,000 shillings*

'SHE WAS LOWERED DOWN THE RIFT VALLEY IN A BASKET AND SAW A HIPPO BITE A BOAT IN HALF'

'A CHICKEN WAS LITERALLY WHAT THEY HAD - AFTER BUYING ONE OFF A NEIGHBOUR AND SLAUGHTERING IT'

- so you'd fill sacks and sacks with money. The Land Rover would be full, and you'd come back with an armed guard by your side. I felt like a gangster!'

But he still felt safe. 'Crime is more opportunistic there, not malicious,' he says. 'People are so happy with so little, but their prerogatives are different. Community stands for everything and hospitality is important, so you'd be invited by the farmers to sit and eat with them - I was even offered a daughter in marriage once!'

Bertie, who is now back in the UK and working for Schluter bean importers says, 'What I did was amazing, but not all that easy. But I've had time to reflect, and all the stuff that used to annoy me - the informality, nothing working, the laid back thing, is what I miss - that approach to life. It's proper living, and it's so life affirming. And I saw the funniest things,' he adds, laughing, 'like a guy going past on a motorbike with the wheel hanging off, and six pigs on the back of it.'

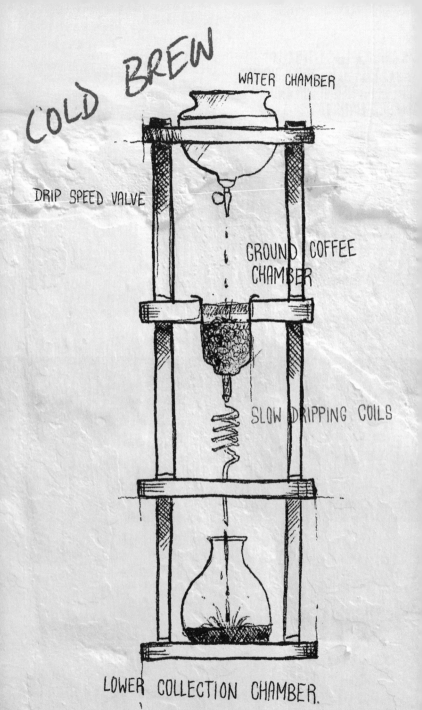

COLD BREW

WATER CHAMBER

DRIP SPEED VALVE

GROUND COFFEE CHAMBER

SLOW DRIPPING COILS

LOWER COLLECTION CHAMBER.

HOW TO USE THE GUIDE

VENUES
These are coffee houses, cafes and mobile coffee vans where you'll be able to drink a top notch cup.

ROASTERS
Meet the leading artisan coffee roasters in the South West and discover where to source beans to use at home.

MORE GOOD CUPS
These are venues that make the grade, but who have chosen not to take space in the guide.

MAPS AND INDEX
Every venue and roaster has a number, so you can find them either on the large map on the next page, or on one of the detailed city maps which we've included to help you track them down more easily.

We've split the South West into counties and cities to help you discover places that are near you. There's also an index at the back of the guide so you can search for businesses by name.

Don't forget to let us know how you get on as you explore the South West's best coffee venues and roasters – 🐦 @indycoffeeguide

YOU ARE
HERE

COFFEE VENUE

ROASTER

MOBILE COFFEE VENUE

MORE GOOD CUPS

DEVON

EXETER
SEE PAGE 77 FOR CITY MAP

CORNWALL

GLOUCESTERSHIRE

BRISTOL
SEE PAGE 54 FOR CITY MAP

BATH
SEE PAGE 45 FOR CITY MAP

WILTSHIRE

SOMERSET

DORSET

Locations are approximate

VENUES

Impeccable places to drink coffee

GLOUCESTERSHIRE

Indy coffee venues

MAP 1. NEW ENGLAND COFFEE HOUSE

1 Digbeth Street, Stow-on-the-Wold, Cheltenham, Gloucestershire, GL54 1BN.

Nearly six years ago, following a dream of owning their own coffee shop, David and Alison Cunliffe took over a three-floored, 370-year-old listed building in the heart of Stow-on-the-Wold in the Cotswolds. As part of the building they also inherited a roaster which *was never part of the dream,'* laughs David.

To his surprise he's embraced it to become fully immersed in the art of coffee roasting and now supplies several other businesses in addition to his own shop. With a mantra of *'doing a few things very well, rather than several things in a mediocre way,'* the couple have intentionally limited their offering to coffee and cake, saying, *'Because we don't do food we have to be the best at coffee.'* Naturally then, the cakes are also pretty damn good and made by Alison using local ingredients. The pair also provide a range of other drinks including teas, smoothies and Italian style hot chocolate.

This is a coffee shop with personality, from the four lounges full of reclaimed and eclectic furnishings, to the house roasted beans and the music (upbeat on Friday and Saturday, more chilled on Sunday). And even if it does mean hundreds of journeys carrying cups of coffee across wonky floors and up endless stairs, David wouldn't have his coffee shop any other way.

KEY ROASTER
Stow Town Coffee

Gluten FREE

BREWING METHODS
Espresso, filter

COFFEE BEANS AVAILABLE

MACHINE
Fracino Contempo

SOYA MILK AVAILABLE

GRINDERS
Ceado E37, Mazzer

WIFI

OPENING HOURS
Mon-Fri
8.30am-5pm
Sat & Sun
9am-5pm

FAMILY FRIENDLY

INSIDER'S TIP HEAD TO THE SECRET LIBRARY LOUNGE ON THE THIRD FLOOR

---

www.newenglandcoffeehouse.co.uk   T: 01451 831171

f New England Coffee House   🐦 @newengcoffeehse

MAP №2. THE COFFEE DISPENSARY

18 Regent Street, Cheltenham, Gloucestershire, GL50 1HE.

Inspired by a trip to Colonna and Small's in Bath, Gary Marshall was blown away by an experience of coffee unlike anything he'd ever drunk before. The seed was sown and two years on, Gary has just opened his Coffee Dispensary in Cheltenham.

Housed in a regency building which was previously home to a working pharmacy, the décor is loosely based on a Scandi theme while sustenance comes in the form of homemade cakes and pastries from local cake maker, Hetty.

With the aim of emulating a little of the coffee alchemy that inspired the Dispensary, Gary's invested in a state-of-the-art Sanremo Opera espresso machine, while filters are carefully made using V60 pourover and Clever dripper, with AeroPress and syphon serves also available. Connoisseurs can indulge in the rotating seasonal, single origin coffees.

KEY ROASTER
Extract

BREWING METHODS
Espresso, V60, AeroPress, Clever dripper, syphon

MACHINE
Sanremo Opera

GRINDERS
EK43, K30

OPENING HOURS
Mon-Fri
8am-5.30pm
Sat 8.30am-5.30pm
Sun 10am-4pm

INSIDER'S TIP HETTY'S TEA PARTY MATCHES THE CAKES TO THE COFFEES' FLAVOUR PROFILES, SO ASK FOR A PERFECT PAIRING

www.the-coffee-dispensary.co.uk   T: 01242 279511

f The Coffee Dispensary   🐦 @coffeedispenser

MAP Nº 3. BREW & BAKE

217 Bath Road, Cheltenham, Gloucestershire, GL53 7NA.

Within six months of opening, Brew & Bake made it into the top five coffee spots in Cheltenham.

Owner Mark Conway is on a roll (ahem), and as a highly experienced chef and coffee fan, he's mixed all the right ingredients to create his first neighbourhood coffee shop. Mark uses roaster Ue Coffee (the only wood roasted coffee company in the UK) as, with 15 other places to grab a cup on his street, it was important to find something a little bit different to offer customers.

Food is a talking point at Brew & Bake, and includes a choice of 15 sandwiches (using Hobbs House bread), along with changing surprises like lasagne muffins, scotch eggs and veggie sausage rolls – and of course those tempting cakes and pastries. Everything's prepared and baked on site, and local suppliers are at the core of the operation, from jam makers to butchers to beer and cider producers – you'll probably spot them popping in for a coffee.

The interior, with its custom reclaimed scaffolding plank tables, coffee sack benches, school chairs and cool artwork, is simple and relaxed, and continually being updated as a result of Mark's keen eye for reclaimed finds.

KEY ROASTER
Ue

BREWING METHODS
Espresso, V60, Chemex

MACHINE
La Marzocco Linea

GRINDER
Super Jolly on demand

OPENING HOURS
Mon-Sat 7am-6pm
Sun 10am-3pm

INSIDER'S TIP CHECK OUT THE IMPRESSIVE HAND DRAWN ILLUSTRATION OF A SECTION OF BATH ROAD

www.brewandbake.coffee   T: 01242 580875

f Brew & Bake   🐦 @brewandbakehq

MAP Nº 4. STAR ANISE ARTS CAFE

1 Gloucester Street, Stroud, Gloucestershire, GL5 1QG.

Star Anise Cafe is one of Stroud's hidden gems. Just off the bustling main street, a very strong ethos courses through its veins, which is to serve up delicious and nourishing seasonal food, freshly made on site every day. This includes dishes like the superfood salad, containing black quinoa, chia seeds, avocado and fresh peach.

Of course, there's no point producing amazing food without serving the finest speciality coffee to go with it, and the cafe's teamed up with Extract to provide its house blend – along with ongoing training for its baristas. It's worth noting it also has a fine selection of local organic and biodynamic wines and beers too, including Stroud Brewery's award-winning organic beer, Budding.

INSIDER'S TIP OYSTER MUSHROOMS USED IN DISHES ARE GROWN USING THE CAFE'S RECYCLED COFFEE GROUNDS

A linchpin of the local community, Star Anise often has live music, art shows and events going on, and this year has been cooking for the UK's first ever vegan football team - Forest Green Rovers. On sunny days the cafe is a great place to hang out, with a warm courtyard and a licensed bar.

KEY ROASTER
Extract

BREWING METHOD
Espresso

MACHINE
Sanremo

GRINDER
Sanremo

OPENING HOURS
Mon-Fri 8am-5pm
Sat 8.30am-5pm

---

www.staraniseartscafe.com   T: 01453 840021

f Star Anise Arts Cafe   🐦 @staranisecafe

5. COTSWOLD ARTISAN COFFEE

5 Bishop's Walk, Cricklade Street, Cirencester, Gloucestershire, GL7 1JH.

There's a massive passion for coffee at Cotswold Artisan Coffee in Cirencester, which is clear as owner Barry Cook reveals the care that goes into each cup. *'I like to deal with customers on a one to one basis,'* explains owner Barry, *'because with speciality coffee you have to spend time with people to find out what brewing method or roast they'd enjoy most.'*

With six single origins and an extensive range of brew methods available, Barry's got lots of options and combinations at his fingertips. He's eager to share his knowledge with the customers too, including explaining the sustainable ethos that runs through the cafe. This autumn, the popular neighbourhood coffee shop will also be teaming up with its key roaster, Union, to host a new series of coffee tasting sessions, with a big launch event followed by smaller, more intimate sessions in the cafe's atrium.

It's not just all about coffee though, and Barry's wife Mandy keeps the handmade bar well stocked with homemade cakes – lots made using ingredients grown in the couple's garden.

KEY ROASTER
Union

BREWING METHODS
Espresso, V60, AeroPress, Chemex, Clever dripper

MACHINE
Wega Concept All Black

GRINDERS
Mazzer Super Jolly, Wega Compak, Macap MC5 deli grinder

OPENING HOURS
Mon-Sat
8am-5.30pm
Sun 10am-3pm
Subject to seasonal change

INSIDER'S TIP TAKE ALONG YOUR OWN EQUIPMENT AND GET SOME PRO KNOW-HOW ON HOW TO MAKE THE BEST COFFEE AT HOME

T: 01285 239327

 @cotsartcoffee

MAP № 6. VELOTON

22 Market Place, Tetbury, Gloucestershire, GL8 8DD.

Across the country, cyclists are planning their routes around their next caffeine fix and fuelling this passion is the meteoric rise of the cycle cafe - serving wonderful speciality coffee and homemade food. If that's your bag, you'll love Veloton.

Having spent years in Australia where the coffee/cycling culture is a big deal, owner Martin wanted to bring a taste of this cycling trend to the beautiful Cotswolds. And serving consistently great coffee using a La Marzocco Linear 3 group, the cafe is nailing its vision.

Martin is acutely aware that cyclists are very on the ball about what they eat and the ingredients used, saying, '*All our produce is of the highest quality: the organic milk is from the local dairy, the fresh juices produced down the road and the cakes homemade. I like to be able to look a cyclist in the eye and tell him where everything has come from.*'

With a fully equipped workshop and Cytech trained mechanic on hand, what better excuse to cruise down for a coffee and a sneaky slice of cake, while your two wheeled love gets a quick once over.

KEY ROASTER
Batch Coffee

BREWING METHOD
Espresso

MACHINE
La Marzocco Linea 3 group

GRINDER
Mahlkonig K30

OPENING HOURS
Mon-Sat
8.30am-5pm
Sun 8.30am-1pm

SOYA MILK AVAILABLE

WIFI

CYCLE FRIENDLY

OUTDOOR SEATING

INSIDER'S TIP CHECK OUT THE INDUSTRIAL, VINTAGE AND RECYCLED ELEMENTS INSIDE

www.veloton.co.uk   T: 01666 504343

f Veloton   🐦 @velotonuk

Speciality coffee
PERFECTLY
CRAFTED

on → *Betty*

OUR HAND RESTORED
1955 VINTAGE ROASTER

EXTRACT
COFFEE
ROASTERS

SHOP & SUBSCRIBE ONLINE

EXTRACTCOFFEE.CO.UK

SOMERSET

with

BATH & BRISTOL

city maps

250

250
ml

200

approx.vol.

150

100

SIMAX
CZECH REPUBLIC

MOKOKO
MAP. № 14 | PAGE. № 53

MoKO

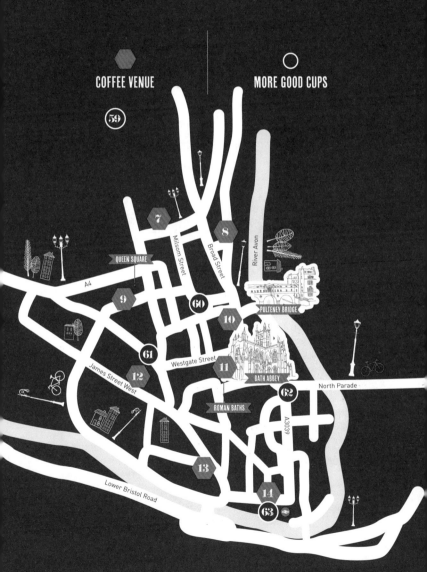

BATH
city centre

COFFEE VENUE

MORE GOOD CUPS

59

7

8

River Avon

Milsom Street

Broad Street

QUEEN SQUARE

A4

9

60

10

PULTENEY BRIDGE

61

Westgate Street

11

BATH ABBEY

James Street West

12

ROMAN BATHS

62

North Parade

A3039

13

Lower Bristol Road

14

63

Locations are approximate

7. CHANDOS DELI

12 George Street, Bath, BA1 2EH.

One of those Bath institutions, the Chandos Deli on George Street, just up the hill from Bath's main shopping centre, is a popular haunt of locals in need of refreshment – some visit up to four times a day!

It's been around for 14 years and has seen a few changes, but current manager, Jhampoll (JP) and his team are on a mission to serve *'the best cup of coffee in Bath'*. The team's coffee expertise is kept up to scratch with the help of Bristol roaster Wogan Coffee, and JP says, *'We all love coffee and when I'm out I'm particularly picky about coffee, so I understand how important it is to our customers.'*

Inside, Chandos is simply furnished with muted tones, tiled walls, high ceilings and lots of wood, plus two striking stained glass windows in the rear seating area.

Visit in the morning for its fabulous range of brekkie items – especially the toast and granolas, while at lunchtime the salads, quiches, soups, wraps and toasties come to the fore. In recent years it's also developed an impressive range of wines, and with an Enomatic Wine Dispenser installed, there are also plenty of excellent choices by the glass.

KEY ROASTER
Wogan

BREWING METHOD
Espresso

MACHINE
Rancillo

GRINDER
Ceado

OPENING HOURS
Mon-Fri
8am-5.30pm
Sat 9am-7pm
Sun 9am-5pm

Gluten FREE

COFFEE BEANS AVAILABLE

SOYA MILK AVAILABLE

WIFI

FAMILY FRIENDLY

INSIDER'S TIP TRY A CHORIZO SAUSAGE ROLL, FRESH FROM THE OVEN'

www.chandosdeli.com   T: 01225 314418

f Chandos Deli   🐦 @chandosdeli

MAP №8. PICNIC COFFEE

9 Saracen Street, Bath, BA1 5BR.

Day or night, it's great to hang out at Picnic – it's one of those coffee shops where you feel bereft if you haven't popped in during the day, the sort of place you find yourself missing when you're on holiday.

Owner Tim Starks has created a continental type venue in the heart of the city, a social hub for both locals and visitors. Picnic's barista of 11 years, Jenn, says, *'It's the ethos behind this place. It's quirky, chilled out and friendly – rather like being in your own home.'*

Since last year the team has installed a fab new espresso machine – a Victoria Arduino Black Eagle – and there's also a new, second Picnic outpost in Bath, offering a varied, made-to-order food menu. Find it upstairs at designer clothes shop Rupert & Buckley on Burton Street.

Whether you're inside on a sofa, or at one of the fold down pavement tables, you'll want to stay a while. Nice items like the library of travel books, tasting notes behind the bar and coffee sack cushions add to the atmosphere, plus Jenn and co are always happy to chat about the excellent range of coffees. It's open late on some nights too, so you can enjoy a glass of wine, craft beer and some music.

KEY ROASTER
Easy José

BREWING METHODS
Espresso, V60 pourover, AeroPress, cold brew in summer

MACHINE
Victoria Arduino Black Eagle

GRINDERS
Mahlkonig K30, Mahlkonig Varios, Compak E8

OPENING HOURS
Mon-Wed
7.30am-6pm
Thurs-Fri
7.30am-9pm
Sat 8.30am-9pm
Sun 9am-5pm

INSIDER'S TIP SUPER DOG FRIENDLY, THIS IS BATH'S POOCH LOVERS' TOP COFFEE STOP

---

www.picniccoffee.co.uk   T: 01225 330128

f Picnic Coffee   🐦 @picnic_bath

MAP № 9. COLONNA & SMALL'S

6 Chapel Row, Bath, BA1 1HN.

BOURBON
SL-28
GEISHA
LONGBERRY
ACAIA
CATUAI
PACAMARA
TYPICA

A mecca for South West speciality coffee lovers, this airy coffee shop on Bath's Queen Square is a science lab, theatre and coffee shop rolled into one.

Spend a little time propping up its brew bar and you'll witness precision and flair in equal measure from Maxwell Colonna-Dashwood's brigade of award winning baristas. Three time UK Barista Champion and three time World Finalist himself, Maxwell has become the coffee geek's coffee geek and "pilgrimage" the only word to describe many customers' experience of their visit.

In the way that leading chefs focus on seasonality of produce, Colonna and Small's focuses on the seasonality of beans, so you'll find different coffees from leading roasteries changing weekly, influenced by the fact that, 'coffee tastes better if you embrace the seasonality of coffee growing'. The team is also beginning to roast coffee inhouse, focusing on the world's rarest and most difficult to source beans.

There's a wide menu of serve styles to experiment with, plus detailed tasting notes to inform your choice.

KEY ROASTER
Round Hill,
Has Bean, Origin,
James Gourmet,
Tate, Workshop

BREWING METHODS
Espresso, lungo
AeroPress, syphon
and Clever dripper
with V60 papers

MACHINE
Sanremo Opera

GRINDER
Mahlkonig EK43

OPENING HOURS
Mon-Wed 8am-5pm
Thurs-Sat
8am-10pm
Sun Closed for now

INSIDER'S TIP TRY COLONNA & HUNTER FOR CRAFT BEER AND COFFEE IN THE CITY TOO

www.colonnaandsmalls.co.uk   T: 07766 808067

f Colonna and Small's   🐦 @colonna_smalls

MAP Nº 10. SOCIETY CAFE

19 High Street, Bath, BA1 5AJ.

With its bare stone, plain walls and big windows, this is the Scandi influenced little sister to Society Cafe in Kingsmead Square.

Close to the cathedral and right in the heart of big chain coffee land, the diminutive little pit stop is a welcome independent speciality coffee outpost.

INSIDER'S TIP
BE SURE TO TRY BEN'S LOCALLY-SMOKED SALMON SARNIE

It's popular with local traders and office workers for a daily caffeine hit takeaway - as well as for its sandwiches, cakes and pastries, but there are bar seats for those who want to chill for a bit and watch the baristas at work. The team here know their coffee and love to chat about the single origin espressos and filters on offer. Local roaster Round Hill features strongly, but there are always guest offerings alongside too.

The ethos is still very much the same as the original venue, reflecting themes that are important to owners Adrian and Jane Campbell-Howard. That means it focuses on no-nonsense food and drinks done exceptionally well, and also on family, friends, connectivity and creativity – the clue's in the name.

KEY ROASTER
Round Hill

BREWING METHODS
Espresso,
AeroPress,
Clever dripper

MACHINE
La Marzocco
Linea PB

GRINDERS
Mahlkonig K30
Twin Vario,
Mahlkonig EK43

OPENING HOURS
Mon-Sat
7.30am-6pm
Sun 10am-6pm

Gluten FREE

COFFEE BEANS AVAILABLE

SOYA MILK AVAILABLE

WIFI

COFFEE COURSES AVAILABLE

www.society-cafe.com   T: 01225 428008

f Society Cafe   @societycafebath

MAP № 11. JACOB'S COFFEE HOUSE

6 Abbey Churchyard, Bath, Somerset, BA1 1LY.

In the city's historic heart, opposite Bath Abbey and the Pump Rooms, Jacob's Coffee House is easy to find, and full of character and charm. Old crate shelves, dark wood, cool blue walls and a leather sofa create atmosphere in this many-roomed and deceptively spacious interior.

INSIDER'S TIP THE 4OZ PICCOLOS ARE SPECIAL – CHOOSE ONE MADE WITH A GUEST SINGLE ESTATE BEAN

More enticement comes from the aroma of coffee - both seasonal blends and guest estates from Ethiopia, Guatemala, Colombia and Peru. You're put in mind of an eighteenth century coffee house, especially when tucking into one of Jacob's famous pie and mash lunches.

While it's enough to simply sit and sample the various coffees with their markedly different cupping signatures, the food is worth the trip alone, and you'll be tempted by the fabulous array of cakes in the window - all made by the inhouse pastry chef. You can also dig into soups and handmade stone-baked ciabatta pannini - try the scrumptious harissa-spiced Italian Hero. There's also a large range of teas and infusions, which, just like the coffee, are selected for quality. Jacob's is the big sister to Mokoko, Bath's new brew bar near the train station.

KEY ROASTER
Easy José

BREWING METHOD
Espresso

MACHINE
Conte Monte Carlo

GRINDERS
Mahlkonig K30
Air x 3

OPENING HOURS
Mon-Sun
8am-6.30pm

www.jacobscoffeehouse.com   T: 01225 758132

f Jacob's Coffee House   🐦 @jacobscoffeehse

12. SOCIETY CAFE

5 Kingsmead Square, Bath, BA1 2AB.

Set in one of the listed Georgian buildings in Kingsmead Square, this well established coffee shop spreads out over an intriguing collection of rooms.

The spacious ground level serving area (you can even wheel a bike through) has big tables, bar stool window seating and there are cosy armchairs in a room to the side. Or head down to the basement where you'll find plenty of room to spread out or little nooks to squirrel away in. The whole place is uncannily Tardis like.

INSIDER'S TIP HUNT DOWN THE BRILLIANT MAP TABLE IN THE BASEMENT

There's always something to look at, with ever-changing artwork on the walls, and a selection of books, so it's easy to while away the hours here. And service is such a big deal that you instantly feel at home: *we love to send customers away happy,* says barista Jay.

One of two Society outlets in the city, this is very much the big sister, and you'll find a concentration on espresso based coffees – with AeroPress and cold brew too. There's also a quality food offering, but coffee remains the focus – and our favourite reason to visit.

KEY ROASTER
Round Hill

BREWING METHODS
Espresso, AeroPress, cold brew

MACHINE
La Marzocco FB80

GRINDERS
Mahlkonig EK43, Mahlkonig Tanzania, Nuova Simonelli Mythos

OPENING HOURS
Mon-Fri
7am-6.30pm
Sat 7.30am-6.30pm
Sun 9am-6pm

 GLUTEN FREE
 COFFEE BEANS AVAILABLE
 SOYA MILK AVAILABLE
 WIFI
 CYCLE FRIENDLY
 OUTDOOR SEATING
 FAMILY FRIENDLY

www.society-cafe.com   T: 01225 442433
f Society Cafe @societycafebath

MAP 13. FORUM COFFEE HOUSE

3-5 Forum Buildings, St James' Parade, Bath, BA1 1UG.

The new kid on the coffee block in Bath is Forum Coffee House.

Just off the Southgate shopping centre at the lower end of town, it's close to Bath College, which may explain why it's gained such a loyal student following. A retreat from the madness of daily life, it's blissfully cool and spacious inside, due to the Art Deco credentials of the Forum Building to which it belongs.

Lounge on a sofa or banquette while you chat over a coffee, or perch on a stool and people-watch from one of the big picture windows. And if you want to get closer to the action you can be entertained by the baristas at work at the central bar area.

The team uses Clifton Coffee for espresso based drinks and has a small range of rotating filter options. '*We love speciality coffee but don't want to alienate people,*' says barista Maisie, so feel free to get advice on what's good. It's a happy team who work here and although it only opened in September 2014, Forum is already building up a community feel – artists and musicians are encouraged to get involved in the shop and by Maisie's reckoning at least 80 per cent of its customers are regulars.

KEY ROASTER
Clifton

BREWING METHODS
Espresso, AeroPress, Chemex, cold brew

MACHINE
La Marzocco Linea PB

GRINDERS
Mahlkonig K30, Tanzania

OPENING HOURS
Mon-Fri 8am-5pm
Sat 9am-6pm
Sun 9am-4pm

INSIDER'S TIP **TRY THE CARROT CAKE – IT'S KNOCK OUT**

www.bathforum.co.uk   T: 01225 443114

f Forum Coffee House   🐦 @bathforumcoffee

14. MOKOKO

7 Dorchester Street, Southgate, Bath, Somerset, BA1 1SS.

This newbie brew bar is - almost quite literally - a window into the world of coffee. Situated opposite Bath Spa train and bus stations, it's the little companion to Jacob's Coffee house. It shares the same warm friendliness of Jacob's but allows the small team of baristas to fully immerse themselves in a few brew methods, including syphon, Chemex and drip.

Mokoko is filled with the latest gear and with its large picture windows, it's no surprise that passers-by have a tendency to stand and watch the baristas at work. Seasonal espresso blends and single estate coffees from around the world are served to suit every palate – you can even pick up a brew guide to help you make better coffee at home.

This is a place for serious - but unpretentious - coffee chat but if you don't want to prop up the brew bar there's also room to sit and relax out on the covered pavement area, with a coffee and one of the fabulous creations made by Jacobs' pastry chef.

KEY ROASTERS
Mokoko, Easy José

BREWING METHODS
Espresso, V60, AeroPress, Chemex, syphon, drip

MACHINE
Conti Monti Carlo

GRINDER
Mahlkonig Twin K30 Air

OPENING HOURS
Mon-Sat 7am-7pm
Sun 9am-6pm

 Gluten FREE
 COFFEE BEANS AVAILABLE
 SOYA MILK AVAILABLE
 WIFI
 CYCLE FRIENDLY
 OUTDOOR seating

INSIDER'S TIP CHECK OUT THE WIDE RANGE OF EQUIPMENT AVAILABLE FOR BUDDING BARISTAS TO BUY

www.mokoko.biz T: 01225 333444
@mokokobath

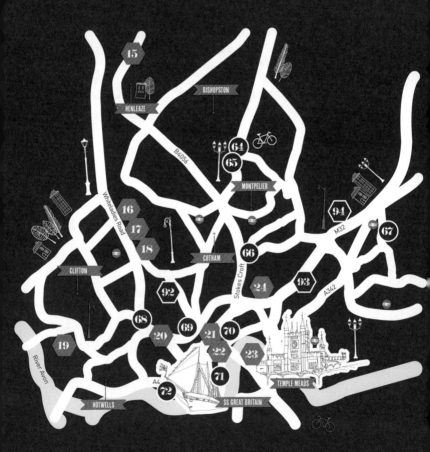

BRISTOL
city centre

COFFEE VENUE   ROASTER   MORE GOOD CUPS

15
HENLEAZE
BISHOPSTON
B4056
64
65
MONTPELIER
16
Whiteladies Road
17
18
COTHAM
CLIFTON
66
Stokes Croft
94
M32
67
93
A342
24
92
68
69
70
20
21
22
23
19
River Avon
71
A4
72
HOTWELLS
SS GREAT BRITAIN
TEMPLE MEADS

Locations are approximate

MAP Nº 15. CHANDOS DELI

97 Henleaze Road, Bristol, BS9 4JP.

To simply talk about the coffee at Chandos Deli in Henleaze would be to do it a massive disservice. This is a cathedral to eating and drinking - from the beautifully crafted and kept French cheeses to the Bertinet and Hobbs House Bakery breads, knobbly garlic saucisson and the basket of fresh tomatoes at the door. And good coffee? That's the icing on the cake.

Talking of cakes, the pastries are exquisite and you couldn't go far wrong on a Saturday morning than to sit in with a pastel de nata portuguese tart and a hand crafted piccolo from either the Kenyan Pea Berry or the single origin, La Bastilla. The beans are roasted by Wogan Coffee in Bristol, and coffees made with milk from local Chew Valley Dairy.

Such South West delights are matched by imported delicacies from all over the world, stacked high on groaning produce shelves. You'll need a second coffee to give you enough time to make your mind up over which goodies you're going to take home with you.

KEY ROASTER
Wogan

BREWING METHOD
Espresso

MACHINE
Rancilio Class 7

GRINDER
Mazzer

OPENING HOURS
Mon-Sat
8am-5pm

Gluten FREE

COFFEE BEANS AVAILABLE

SOYA MILK AVAILABLE

CYCLE FRIENDLY

OUTDOOR seating

FAMILY FRIENDLY

INSIDER'S TIP VISIT ON SATURDAYS FOR GOURMET TASTINGS FROM AROUND THE GLOBE

---

www.chandosdeli.com   T: 01179 074391

f Chandos Deli   🐦 @chandosdeli

MAP No. 16. TRADEWIND ESPRESSO

118 Whiteladies Road, Bristol, BS8 2RP.

The little sister cafe to roastery Roasted Rituals Coffee, Tradewind Espresso threw its doors open on Whiteladies Road in September 2015.

In creating the cafe, founders Patrick and Tahi Grant-Sturgis had a vision to create the kind of communal venue they love to eat at and drink coffee in. And when you look at the little details the pair have drawn inspiration from, it's clear they have applied the same standards to this new business, as they do to coffee roasting. Tahi states proudly that they set out to produce, *'coffee with character, food with flavour, served in vibrant nutritious dishes that inspire.'*

Using their own coffee, they'll regularly rotate custom blends and single origins, and complement with only the freshest seasonal produce on the menu. Tahi continues, *'If we can make food from scratch we will, and the cakes, nut milks, preserves, smoked fish, salt beef and salads are prepared daily on site.'*

Going by early reviews, Tradewind looks set to inspire a loyal following, especially among coffee fiends who know of Roasted Rituals. So if you're in Bristol, this new cafe is definitely worth a visit.

KEY ROASTER
Roasted Rituals

BREWING METHODS
Espresso, V60, french press

MACHINE
La Marzocco Linea PB

GRINDERS
Mazzer Robur x2, EK43

OPENING HOURS
Mon-Sat 8am-5pm
Sun 9am-4pm

INSIDER'S TIP TRADE WINDS ARE AN EASTERLY WIND PATTERN WHICH MARINERS USED TO SAIL COFFEE FROM THE TROPICS TO EUROPE

---

www.tradewindespresso.com   T: 07855 380561

f Tradewind Espresso   🐦 @tradewind118

17. BRISTOL COFFEE HOUSE

121 Whiteladies Road, Clifton, Bristol, BS8 2PL.

Part of the Chandos family, Bristol Coffee House is the super caffeinated little brother, focusing on quality coffee first and foremost, at its Whiteladies Road location.

Get stuck into the Nicaraguan single origin, La Bastilla, a medium roast, well rounded cup with hazelnut and chocolate flavours, with good acidity. Roasted by the city's Wogan Coffee, it's complemented by guest single origins from across the world.

As befits the focus on coffee, you can take your morning cup in a number of serve styles including AeroPress, cold brew, and of course espresso – and everything that comes with it.

Join the regulars from local offices and media businesses getting their coffee fix with a slab of banana bread or a toastie, and sit out front on sunny days and enjoy watching the world go by in this vibrant part of town.

INSIDER'S TIP RIGHT NEXT DOOR TO COSTA COFFEE, CHOOSING THIS INDEPENDENT IS DAILY STATEMENT OF SUPPORT FOR "LOCAL"

KEY ROASTER
Wogan

BREWING METHODS
Espresso, cold brew, pourover, AeroPress

MACHINE
La Marzocco Linea

GRINDER
Compak K10 RS Barista Pro

OPENING HOURS
Mon-Fri 7am-5pm
Sat 8am-6pm
Sun 9am-5pm

Gluten FREE

COFFEE BEANS AVAILABLE

SOYA MILK AVAILABLE

WIFI

CYCLE FRIENDLY

OUTDOOR SEATING

FAMILY FRIENDLY

COFFEE COURSES AVAILABLE

www.bristolcoffeehouse.co.uk   T: 01179 706565

f Bristol Coffee House   🐦 @bristolcoffeehouse

MAP Nº 18. BREW COFFEE CO

45 Whiteladies Road, Bristol, BS8 2LS.

N ow well into its second year, this home-grown coffee shop on Whiteladies Road has a loyal following.

Brew is the result of owner Matt Atkins' many years of working in the coffee industry. A rich store of knowledge, gleaned from working with both chains and independents - plus bar and restaurant work in the UK and in Australia, was filtered, percolated and extracted to create his first coffee shop.

Matt's found a plum location right alongside the BBC TV studios, so it's popular with office workers wanting a quick coffee and bite to eat, as well as for its legendary bunches at the weekend. Wood, white walls, work by local artists and upcycled furniture create a natural, authentic feel and

INSIDER'S TIP THE BOURBON CUSTARD CROISSANT CAKE HAS A BIG FOLLOWING

alongside top notch coffee, there's a superb food offering, including frittata, pastries, colourful salads and juices, all freshly prepared on the premises. But don't just take our word for it - Brew has also won the Bristol Good Food Award for Best Cafe Food. *'We want people to walk through the door and feel they want to hang out here,'* says Matt. *'It's simple really, Brew is about relaxation, eating quality food and experiencing a brilliant brew.'*

KEY ROASTER
Clifton

BREWING METHODS
Filter, espresso

MACHINE
La Marzocco Linea

GRINDER
Mazzer

OPENING HOURS
Mon-Fri
7.30am-6.30pm
Sat 8am-6.30pm
Sun 9am-6pm

Gluten FREE

COFFEE BEANS AVAILABLE

SOYA MILK AVAILABLE

WIFI

CYCLE FRIENDLY

OUTDOOR SEATING

FAMILY FRIENDLY

DISABLED ACCESS

www.brewcoffeecompany.co.uk   T: 01179 732842

f Brew Coffee Company   🐦 @brewcc

19. SPICER+COLE

9 Princess Victoria Street, Clifton Village, Bristol, BS8 4BX.

With two outlets in the city, Spicer+Cole is worth tracking down for great coffee and some stonking food. A groaning bar of cakes, salads, pastries and interesting breads is drop dead gorgeous – deciding what to order the only problem.

You could start the day here in style with a bacon and poached egg bap with homemade harissa and aioli, stay on for lunch of one of its tarts or tortillas of the day with an array of interesting salads, and languish into the afternoon over tea and tray bakes or a big slab of coffee cake.

INSIDER'S TIP VISIT FOR HOUSE COLD BREW IN THE SUMMER MONTHS

Of course, coffee is de rigeur whatever the time of day, and with the house roast made by Bristol's Extract, you're in safe hands. The coffees are all espresso based and guest espressos also feature (as does almond milk and soya), complemented by hot chocolate and babyccinos to keep everyone happy.

Visit the sister cafe on Queen Square too – it's equally good and you can walk off your overindulgence with a stroll along the river.

KEY ROASTER
Extract

BREWING METHOD
Espresso

MACHINE
Sanremo TCS

GRINDERS
Mahlkonig,
Sanremo

OPENING HOURS
Mon-Fri
7.30am-5.30pm
Sat-Sun
8.30am-5.30pm

www.spicerandcole.co.uk   T: 01179 732485

f Spicer and Cole   🐦 @spicerandcole

MAP 20. BOSTON TEA PARTY

75 Park Street, Bristol, BS1 5PF.

BTP Park Street was the first cafe in the family owned, independent group, and is still its flagship store.

As a stalwart of the speciality coffee scene in Bristol over the last 20 years, it's been enticing coffee drinkers away from the national and international chains and drawing them in for its appealing offer of great coffee (from Bristol's Extract), made with locally sourced milk and complemented by good quality, authentic cafe food which ranges from doorstep sarnies to homemade soups, big breakfasts, smoothies and hearty cakes – with everything made on-site. As a result it's been awarded a number of gongs including a top three star award by The Sustainable Restaurant Association and *Food* magazine's Best Cafe Award 2015.

There are now five BTP cafes in Bristol (Clifton Village, Whiteladies Road, Gloucester Road and Stokes Croft) and while the coffee scene has evolved from where BTP first started, they've kept pace, introducing guest roasts and regularly changing filter coffees as well as putting a lot of emphasis on barista training and skills.

KEY ROASTER
Extract

BREWING METHODS
Espresso, filter

MACHINE
Nuova Simonelli

GRINDER
Mazzer Major

OPENING HOURS
Mon-Sat 7am-8pm
Sun 8am-7pm

 Gluten FREE

 COFFEE BEANS AVAILABLE

 SOYA MILK AVAILABLE

 WIFI

 CYCLE FRIENDLY

 OUTDOOR seating

FAMILY friendly

INSIDER'S TIP CHOOSE FROM THE MEDIUM AND DARK HOUSE ROASTS, AS WELL AS REGULARLY CHANGING FILTER BLENDS

www.bostonteaparty.co.uk   T: 01179 298601

f Boston Tea Party Cafes   🐦 @btpcafes

SOURCE | ROAST | TEACH | BREW

ORIGIN COFFEE ROASTERS

Centres in Cornwall and London

MAP Nº 21. SMALL STREET ESPRESSO

23 Small Street, Bristol, BS1 1DW.

The closure of a cash machine next door during the past year has allowed Small Street Espresso to extend its interior by about eight feet – which is a lot when, as the name suggests, this is one of Bristol's tiniest espresso bars. However, good things come in small packages and – as bean freak Bristolians well know – the coffee that's pulled through Small Street Espresso's sky-blue La Marzocco is *really* good. Along with the house espresso from Clifton, there's a rotating selection of guest espressos from the likes of Square Mile, Nude and Extract, plus useful tasting notes on the wall.

While they take coffee very seriously here, the vibe is cosy and relaxed with exposed brick walls, a little corner of seating inside and handmade benches out the front on which you can perch while you watch the world go by. Complement your coffee hit with freshly made sourdough sarnies and locally made cakes and sweet treats.

And, if it's one of *those* mornings, ask for a Hit and Go – a £3.50 shot of guest espresso while you wait, with a flat white or piccolo to go (you won't find it on the menu!).

KEY ROASTER
Clifton

BREWING METHODS
Espresso, cold brew, AeroPress

MACHINE
La Marzocco
FB-80

GRINDERS
Mythos x 2

OPENING HOURS
Mon-Fri
7.30am-4.30pm
Sat 9.30am-4.30pm

INSIDER'S TIP CATCH UP ON THE COFFEE NEWS FROM THE SELECTION OF CAFFEINATED READING MATERIAL INSIDE

www.smallstreetespresso.co.uk

f Small St. Espresso 🐦 @smallstespresso

22. PLAYGROUND COFFEE HOUSE

45 St Nicholas Street, Bristol, BS1 1TP.

It's most certainly playtime for coffee lovers at this diminutive central Bristol coffee house. For in addition to the board games and the swings which double as seating for customers, it's the quirky and playful approach to coffee that's so entertaining.

Co-owner Fabian and fellow barista Tommy are hard core caffeine geeks who delight in playing around with all sorts of different beans and serve styles - including the dramatic glowing syphon, various filter methods and through their customised espresso machine. There are also different guest espressos and two or three guest filter coffees on the menu at any time.

Fabian's partner Lilly plays a key part too and says it was her experience of growing up in Greece, with its culture of whiling away the hot midday hours over coffee and games that influenced what they wanted to achieve in Bristol.

Don't go looking for lunch though, as this experience is all about the coffee – albeit with a cake or brownie. Instead luxuriate in coffee chat and a carefully crafted cup - with a go on the swings as a bonus.

KEY ROASTER
Roasted Rituals

BREWING METHODS
Espresso, V60, AeroPress, syphon

MACHINE
La Marzocco Linea

GRINDERS
Mahlkonig K30 Twin, Mahlkonig Columbia, Mahlkonig Vario

OPENING HOURS
Mon-Fri 8am-6pm
Sat 10.30am-6.30pm
Sun 11.30pm-4.30pm

Gluten FREE

COFFEE BEANS AVAILABLE

SOYA MILK AVAILABLE

WIFI

CYCLE FRIENDLY

OUTDOOR seating

FAMILY friendly

COFFEE COURSES AVAILABLE

DISABLED ACCESS

INSIDER'S TIP THE TEAM HAS JUST LAUNCHED A MONTHLY COFFEE CLUB WHERE YOU GET UNLIMITED COFFEE FOR £50

---

www.playgroundcoffee.co.uk   T: 01173 290720

f Playground Coffee House   🐦 @playgroundcofco

MAP № 23. CITY DELI

32 Victoria Street, Bristol, BS1 6BX.

A large and airy coffee shop come cafe, City Deli has become an intrinsic part of the landscape and the lives of local office workers since it opened in 2014. Its long communal tables are usually buzzing with bods on laptops, fuelling their brainpower with coffee and cafe style food, while others come in for take-out.

We'd recommend starting the day as you mean to go on with free-range eggy french toast with smoked bacon and maple syrup or a deli breakfast box of bacon, sausage, mushroom, egg, tomato and toast with a coffee.

Then for lunch it's all about the freshly made sarnies, wraps and take-away/eat-in trays of dishes such as Vietnamese style noodles, with an array of cakes on the big bar for an afternoon sugar fix.

Local sourcing is high on the agenda here and soups, sarnies and salads are all made inhouse with bread from nearby Proper Bread of Montpelier, meats from local butchers John Shepherds and fruit and veg from Total Produce. In the same vein, coffee is provided by local roaster Clifton Coffee and served as espresso based drinks.

KEY ROASTER
Clifton

BREWING METHOD
Espresso

MACHINE
La Spaziale

GRINDER
Mazzer

OPENING HOURS
Mon-Fri
7am-6pm
Sat 9am-3pm

INSIDER'S TIP FORGOT YOUR READING MATTER? CATCH UP ON THE ADVENTURES OF DESPERATE DAN AND CO ON THE DECOUPAGE FURNITURE

www.citydelibristol.co.uk T: 01179 250758

f City Deli 🐦 @citydelibristol

24. BEARPIT SOCIAL

Container 1, St James Barton Underpass (The Bearpit), Bristol, BS1 3LE.

The funky regeneration of the big roundabout that's fondly known as the Bearpit is a definite must-visit in Bristol. Vibrant graffiti and artwork, the big Bearritos bus, and its very own greengrocer, Bear Fruit, are all big draws, but for the coffee lover, it's all about the Bearpit Social. This groovy coffee kiosk with outdoor seating is a fave whatever the weather.

Park up your bike and ask Miriam and Simon to craft you one of their single origin coffees sourced from the city's Wogan Coffee, and accompany it with a toastie, cake or any of its ciabattas made fresh on site each day.

Bearpit Social is known for its espresso based coffees (with two varieties going at any time), *'but ask nicely,'* says Miriam, *'and we'll rustle up an AeroPress or a V60 for you.'* Things are taking off here, and in addition to the themed food days, (Asian Tuesdays and Moroccan Thursdays, since you ask), there are potential markets and a skate ramp in the offing. Why be a stranger, when you can be social?

KEY ROASTER
Wogan

BREWING METHODS
Espresso, V60, AeroPress

MACHINE
Astoria

GRINDER
Mazzer

OPENING HOURS
Mon-Fri
7am-4pm
Sat 9am-4pm

INSIDER'S TIP MAKE LIKE BEARPIT SOCIAL'S REGULAR WHO ASKS THEM TO SURPRISE HIM WITH A DIFFERENT COFFEE SERVE EACH DAY

www.bearpitsocial.co.uk   T: 07738 820393

f Bearpit Social   🐦 @bearpitsocial

MAP № 25. YEO VALLEY HQ

Rhodyate, Blagdon, Bristol, BS40 7YE.

For a slice of urban cool in the heart of the Somerset countryside, head to Yeo Valley HQ (YVHQ) near Bristol.

As the name suggests, this is the foodie venue at the heart of the Yeo Valley dairy operation and, as you'd expect, it's been designed with the same care and attention that marks out this innovative company.

The very funky and spacious restaurant/cafe was originally the staff canteen – it still is, but now members of the public are welcome too, and you'll have the chance to experience coffee from Extract, as well as some very good, rustic, wholesome food including a drop-dead-gorgeous roast on Wednesdays.

INSIDER'S TIP WE RECOMMEND THE AFFOGATO – AN ESPRESSO SHOT POURED OVER A SCOOP OF YEO VALLEY ICE CREAM

It's worth a visit for the views too, as YVHQ is set up high, tucked on the edge of the Mendip Hills and overlooking the glorious valley – you might even spot one of the farm's cows grazing beside the distant lake.

KEY ROASTER
Extract

BREWING METHODS
Espresso, filter

MACHINE
S5 Compact ED
Group 2

GRINDER
Mazzer Lux

OPENING HOURS
Mon-Fri
10am-4pm

 Gluten FREE

 SOYA MILK AVAILABLE

 WIFI

 CYCLE FRIENDLY

 OUTDOOR seating

 FAMILY friendly

 DISABLED ACCESS

---

www.yeovalleyvenues.co.uk   T: 01761 463366

f Yeo Valley   🐦 @yeovalley

MAP Nº 26. STRANGERS WITH COFFEE

31 St Cuthbert Street, Wells, Somerset, BA5 2AW.

Never one to stand still, Ivan Hewitt is on a permanent mission to expand his already considerable coffee knowledge, so it's no surprise to discover he and chef wife Susan are still grabbing the occasional coffee road trip. *'We try and get around,'* he says. *'It's good to see what people are roasting.'*

Although there's a variety of guest beans on the Strangers list – including Clifton, Extract and Round Hill – the key offering comes from Allpress in the shape of its new air roasted beans. *'The roaster is a great piece of kit, and there's only two or three of them around,'* says Ivan.

Another thing they're on to here is fusion food, so expect some new offerings from Susan who's already gathered a following for her menus, which include crushed avocado on sourdough toast with chilli and poached egg. This friendly coffee shop in Somerset's little city is a perfect venue for coffee morning chats where reps from roasteries pop in for a natter about beans with Ivan and his coffee fan customers. Refreshment is not just for human's either; take your pooch to the courtyard for water and free biscuits.

KEY ROASTER
Allpress

BREWING METHODS
Espresso, V60, pourover, syphon, AeroPress, cold brew

MACHINE
La Marzocco Linea

GRINDERS
Mazzer Kony, Super Jolly Vario

OPENING HOURS
Mon-Sat
8am-4.30pm
Sun occasionally
(check Facebook)

INSIDER'S TIP LOOK OUT FOR THE PIE AND CRAFT ALE NIGHTS, WHERE FOOD IS MATCHED TO GLASTONBURY ALES

T: 07728 047233

f Strangers With Coffee

DORSET
& WILTSHIRE
Indy coffee venues

SOULSHINE
MAP.№32 | PAGE.№74

27. GREENGAGES CAFE

31 Catherine Street, Salisbury, Wiltshire, SP1 2DQ.

When Richard Coleman set up his coffee house and restaurant in the heart of historic Salisbury, he wanted to make the coffee offering the best it could be – which is probably why he's got such an enthusiastic barista in the form of Joe Belsey. '*I am a coffee geek*,' confesses Joe, who arrived at Greengages with five years' barista experience.

The pair are on a mission to spread the word about speciality coffee and their passion is infectious. '*There are so many variables*,' Richard enthuses, '*from the farm to when it's packed – and there needs to be so much attention to detail*.' Indeed it's all about the detail at Greengages, and the team use Round Hill beans and an increasing variety of brew methods – including V60, Clever dripper and AeroPress, as well as espresso based coffees. Their efforts are clearly winning them fans, both loyal locals and visitors in search of speciality coffee. The food offering is also impressive, and the gluten free and veggie menu is highly acclaimed. Laid out over two floors in a Grade II-listed building, there's plenty of room to relax, or you can escape to the courtyard area out back on sunny, summer days.

KEY ROASTER
Round Hill

BREWING METHODS
Espresso, V60,
AeroPress,
Clever dripper, filter

MACHINE
La Marzocco
PB3

GRINDERS
Baratza, Mazzer

OPENING HOURS
Mon-Fri
8am-5.30pm
Sat 8am-5pm
Sun Closed

INSIDER'S TIP THERE ARE 15 DIFFERENT CAKES ON AT ANY TIME

www.greengagessalisbury.co.uk　T: 01722 349934

f Greengages Coffeehouse & Restaurant

28. CAFE BOSCANOVA

650 Christchurch Road, Boscombe, Dorset, BH1 4BP.

Situated on Boscombe High Street you'll find Boscanova, an Aladdin's cave of coffee fuelled good times, great music and an even better atmosphere.

There's always something new to catch the eye here whether it's your first or fifth visit, as the walls and ceiling are filled with interesting ephemera. Set up by Joel almost a decade ago, it's easy to see why this pioneer of the coffee shop world is so popular. With a constant stream of customers who know the staff by name, lively global music and of course the sounds and smells of fresh coffee being brewed, Boscanova seems to effortlessly cater to all walks of life, while still retaining a cool coffee vibe.

Food is a core part of the offering and new chef Jim Hayward has been tweaking, refining and putting his own slant on the wonderful menus which include faves like pancakes, wraps and the best breakfast for miles around. As well as branching out into consultancy work, the coffee team here has also started roasting its own beans, something that has been long awaited by local customers – and the staff alike!

KEY ROASTER
Multiple

BREWING METHODS
Espresso, Marco shuttle brewer

MACHINE
La Marzocco
2 group PID

GRINDER
Mazzer, manual, on demand

OPENING HOURS
Mon-Fri 8am-4pm
Sat 8am-5pm
Sun 9am-4pm

INSIDER'S TIP ASK THE TEAM TO RECOMMEND COFFEES AND BITES FROM THE MENU THEY'RE ENJOYING THAT DAY

www.boscanova.com   T: 01202 395596

f Cafe Boscanova   🐦 @cafeboscanova

29. SOUTH COAST ROAST

24 Richmond Hill, Bournemouth, Dorset, BH2 6EJ.

Regulars at South Coast Roast (SCR) have loved this place since it launched with a still-talked-about party two years ago.

SCR is the sister shop to Bournemouth coffee pioneer, Boscanova, and it's where the staff train – along with members of the public who are looking to gain and improve on their coffee skills.

With single cup brews and guest espressos on offer, you'll be hard pushed to find something you don't enjoy here – and that includes the food. Just like the coffee, the emphasis is on speed and deliciousness, with a new menu introduced by Boscanova's head chef, Jim Hayward.

And remember the coffee roaster that was situated in the main window? It's now being put to good use as the Boscanova boys and girls have started roasting their own coffee – with the single origin brews available to try at both venues.

KEY ROASTER
Multiple

BREWING METHODS
Espresso, Marco shuttle, Chemex, Clever french press, V60, cold brew, AeroPress

MACHINE
La Marzocco 2 grp

GRINDERS
Anfim, Mazzer

OPENING HOURS
Mon-Fri 8am-5pm
Sat and Sun 10am-4pm

INSIDER'S TIP LOOK OUT FOR THE POP-UP EVENTS – FROM FORAGED FOOD EVENINGS TO DJ NIGHTS – THEY'RE USUALLY PACKED OUT

---

www.boscanova.com T: 01202 551197

f South Coast Roast 🐦 @southcoastroast

30. ESPRESSO KITCHEN

69 Commercial Road, The Triangle, Bournemouth, Dorset, BH2 5RT.

'*Our mission is simple*,' says Francesca Silvestre, owner of Espresso Kitchen. '*We want to offer the best organic coffee possible, coupled with personal service and cool tunes – it's all about taking the pretentiousness out of speciality coffee.*'

Located in The Triangle, in the heart of Bournemouth, Espresso Kitchen happily meets this mission and is anything but pretentious – instead the vibe is fun, quirky and bohemian, in a funky interior packed to the rafters with an eclectic mix of the '*old, new, arty and nutty*,' as Francesca puts it.

Dorset roaster Bean Press provides the seasonal house blend, while rotating guest coffee is sourced from the likes of Origin and Alchemy. Dig in to one of the homemade cakes too, including vegan and gluten-free options, or try one of the smoothies or huge variety of teas.

And if the organic, fair trade, locally roasted and expertly brewed coffee isn't enough to keep you coming back, then the ever-changing décor of vintage posters and edgy street art, along with the friendly welcome, certainly will.

KEY ROASTER
Bean Press

BREWING METHOD
Espresso

MACHINE
La Marzocco fb70

GRINDER
Luigi Mazzer

OPENING HOURS
Mon-Sat 7am-7pm
Sun 10am-6pm

INSIDER'S TIP ESPRESSO KITCHEN IS A BLAST OF SUMMERTIME, EVEN IN THE DEPTHS OF WINTER

---

www.espressokitchen.co.uk   T: 01202 972420

f Espresso Kitchen Bournemouth   🐦 @expressokitchen

№31. COFFEE SALOON

9 Haven Road, Canford Cliffs, Poole, Dorset, BH13 7LE.

Visitors to Poole who are searching for the perfect brew will definitely want to stop by the fast growing Coffee Saloon. The brainchild of Colin Cross of The Dancing Goat, this mini chain is expanding throughout the South and offering a unique experience.

From the saddles hanging from the ceiling to the exposed brick, corrugated iron details and original church pew seats, the style is mostly reclaimed rustic, so it feels like it's always been a part of the community. It's homely, and not just because you'll receive a warm welcome from the Saloon guys and girls.

INSIDER'S TIP CHECK OUT THE SISTER SALOONS ON THE OLD HIGH STREET AND IN WAREHAM

The layout is deliberately designed to encourage customers to chat among themselves, make new friends and have a yarn with a stranger over a wildly good flat white: 'we like the idea that people can talk to one another here,' says Colin.

With some original Western style food to complement the coffee, swing by – you won't be disappointed.

KEY ROASTER
Origin

BREWING METHOD
Espresso

MACHINE
La Marzocco
Linear PB5

GRINDERS
Mahlkonig EK43,
Nuova Simonelli
Mythos,
Mazzer E

OPENING HOURS
Mon-Fri 7am-5pm
Sat 8am-5pm
Sun 9am-3pm

www.coffeesaloon.com T: 07973 642466

f Coffee Saloon 🐦 @coffeesaloon

32. SOULSHINE

76 South Street, Bridport, Dorset, DT6 3NN.

If you're looking for a relaxed, funky space for good coffee and wholesome food, you'll find it in Bridport's Soulshine cafe.

One of the few places in town open seven days a week, Sundays embody the relaxed vibe of the place – order from the reduced Sunday menu, including all-day breakfasts and, of course, quality coffee.

An arty feel pervades, thanks to work from graffiti artist Xenz and a blackboard menu decorated with butterflies. And when you chill out in the sunny courtyard there's a fence painted with birds and leaves, as well as bookshelves stocked with graphic novels and magazines. Kids can let loose in the play area with vintage Fisher Price toys.

Alongside the house espresso from Extract, you'll find a range of guest coffees, including beans from Amid Giants & Idols, Union, Origin, Rounton, Clifton and Square Mile. The team also creates a range of juices, smoothies, and healthy wholesome foods such as the raw vegan beetroot caramel slice (really good). All bread is baked inhouse, and you'll want to take something home from the deli, natch.

KEY ROASTER
Extract

BREWING METHODS
Espresso, AeroPress

MACHINE
Sanremo Verona TCS

GRINDERS
Mahlkonig K30 Vario Air, Sanremo SR50

OPENING HOURS
Mon-Sat 9am-5pm
Sun 10am-4pm

Gluten FREE

COFFEE BEANS AVAILABLE

SOYA MILK AVAILABLE

WIFI

OUTDOOR seating

FAMILY friendly

DISABLED & ACCESS

INSIDER'S TIP TRY THE VEGGIE BREAKFAST SERVED WITH HOMEMADE BUTTERNUT SQUASH FARL BREAD – THE REGULARS RAVE ABOUT IT

www.soulshinecafe.co.uk   T: 01308 422821

f Soulshine Cafe   @soulshinecafe

33. AMID GIANTS & IDOLS

59 Silver Street, Lyme Regis, Dorset, DT7 3HR.

Amid all the fossil hunting that takes place in the historic harbour town of Lyme Regis, we'd choose this find of a coffee house over an ammonite, any day.

Its unusual moniker is an anagram of owner Xanne's two nieces' names and is indicative of the quirky and independent spirit that runs through the bijou coffee house and micro-roastery.

With Xanne – a UK Barista Championship semi-finalist in 2013 – at the helm, it's clearly in expert hands. Since opening three years ago, Xanne and team have dedicated every waking moment to developing their coffee offering and sourcing, roasting and serving lip-smacking coffees with maximum aroma, flavour profile and freshness. To do that, Xanne's fully committed to finding beans that are ethically sourced: *'Coffee's provenance, quality, producers and a sustainable future for the farmers are what matters,'* she says, *'but most of all, I thrive on seeing people getting excited by speciality coffee.'*

Discover three espresso and two filter options, which are changed every month or so.

KEY ROASTER
Amid Giants & Idols

BREWING METHODS
Espresso,
AeroPress,
pour over, syphon,
wood neck,
cold brew

MACHINE
Marzocco Linea

GRINDERS
Various Mazzers

OPENING HOURS
Mon-Sun Please
check website for
current hours

INSIDER'S TIP TRY A COFFEE AND BREW METHOD FROM THE HAND BREW SECTION

---

www.amidgiantsandidols.com   T: 07928 790254

f Amid Giants & Idols   🐦 @amidgiantsidols

DEVON

with

EXETER
city map

BAYARDS COVE INN

MAP.№42 | PAGE.№86

EXETER

city centre

COFFEE VENUE

ROASTER

MORE GOOD CUPS

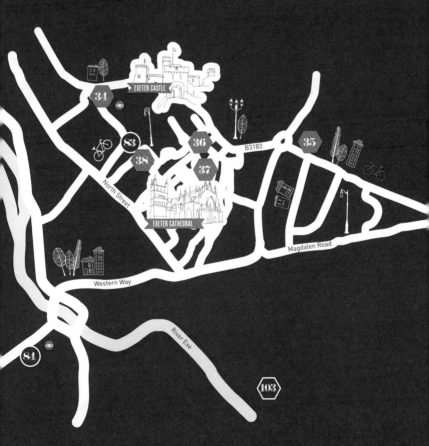

^{MAP}34. THE EXPLODING BAKERY

1B Central Station Buildings, Queen Street, Exeter, Devon, EX4 3SB.

The Exploding Bakery has a secret weapon – the potent and intoxicating aroma of freshly baked cakes and pastries wafting from its cool bakehouse and cafe in central Exeter. If the smell of the incredible edibles doesn't pull you into the cafe, its reputation for superb coffee definitely will, and is why The Exploding Bakery has become a peoples' favourite in the city.

Owner Oliver Coysh and his team of highly skilled bakers and baristas apply the same level of passion and diligence to the coffee as to the cakes. Expect to find interesting guest roasts on offer from Campbell & Syme, Clifton Coffee, Square Mile and Assembly, all carefully sourced to complement its popular Monmouth house blend. Top quality milk is used too: organic and non-homogenised from local Ashclyst Dairy.

Pair a coffee with one of the speciality house tray bakes – the gluten free almond brownie is legendary. Whether you're grabbing a coffee and pastry for breakfast or an afternoon perk-up, The Exploding Bakery should definitely be on your hit list.

KEY ROASTER
Monmouth

BREWING METHODS
Espresso, V60, AeroPress

MACHINE
La Marzocco Linea

GRINDERS
2 x Victoria Arduino Mytho, Mazzer Super Jolly

OPENING HOURS
Mon-Fri 8am-4pm
Sat 9am-4pm
Sun Closed for now

Gluten FREE

COFFEE BEANS AVAILABLE

SOYA MILK AVAILABLE

WIFI

CYCLE FRIENDLY

OUTDOOR SEATING

DISABLED ACCESS

INSIDER'S TIP ORDER THE TECHNO COFFEE FOR INTERESTING FLAVOURS – IT'S USUALLY A HIGHER GRADED BEAN THAN THE (ALREADY GOOD) HOUSE ROAST

www.explodingbakery.com T: 01392 427900

f The Exploding Bakery 🐦 @explodingbakery

№35. EXE COFFEE ROASTERS

19 Heavitree Road, Exeter, Devon, EX1 2LD.

Exe Coffee Roasters (XCR) - is the roasting arm of Devon Coffee, the independent coffee shop based in the centre of Exeter.

XCR roasts all the stock for Devon Coffee, including a range of espresso and single origin filter from the best of the season's crop, on a small coffee roaster that owner Steve built himself. You can also buy its freshly roasted coffee from the website.

INSIDER'S TIP LOOK OUT FOR THE TRAINING COURSES INCLUDING THE POPULAR BE A BARISTA COURSE

Currently under construction (and due to open by December 2015) is XCR's new Exeter coffee shop and retail roastery on Heavitree Road.

Visit to enjoy all the latest coffees which have been roasted onsite and take in the ambience of a working roastery.

The shop is on two floors with the roastery based at ground level and the coffee shop at street level, with seating for 40 people.

The XCR coffee shop and roastery will also continue to run the training courses currently offered by Devon Coffee including the popular Be a Barista course.

KEY ROASTER
XCR

BREWING METHODS
Espresso, V60, AeroPress, filter

MACHINE
La Marzocco Linea

GRINDER
EK43

OPENING HOURS
Mon-Sat 8am-4pm

Gluten FREE

COFFEE BEANS AVAILABLE

SOYA MILK AVAILABLE

WIFI

CYCLE FRIENDLY

OUTDOOR seating

FAMILY FRIENDLY

COFFEE COURSES AVAILABLE

DISABLED ACCESS

---

www.execoffeeroasters.co.uk   T: 07795 105250

f ExeCoffeeRoasters   🐦 @execoffeeroast

MAP N° 36. ARTIGIANO ESPRESSO BAR

248 High Street, Exeter, Devon, EX4 3PZ.

After just a year in the city, Artigiano has already become a destination for coffee drinkers, prosecco sippers and lunchtime feasters in Exeter.

With a prime position on the bustling High Street, the eye-catching glass frontage hints at the super sleek design inside this spacious cafe, bar and eatery. You'll spy all walks of life here, from busy mums chatting over Origin lattes to the city's workforce grabbing artisan baguettes to-go.

Venture inside and it's obvious how passionate the team here is about coffee. The separate brew bar is home to a gleaming La Marzocco Linea machine and a recipe for the perfect shot takes pride of place on the wall behind it.

INSIDER'S TIP
ORDER AN OVEN ROASTED CAMEMBERT TO SHARE FOR AN EVENING TREAT

Open 'til late throughout the week, you'll find a bar vibe at Artigiano come 6pm, with craft beers and ciders, fine wines and pizza sharing boards replacing the sandwiches and smoothies. With the baristas crafting cups till close, head here for the only speciality coffee in the city past tea time.

KEY ROASTER
Origin

BREWING METHOD
Espresso

MACHINE
La Marzocco
Linea PB

GRINDER
Mazzer Major

OPENING HOURS
Mon-Wed
7.30am-8pm
Thurs-Sat
7.30am-11.30pm
Sun 10am-6pm

www.artigiano.uk.com   T: 01392 499169

f Artigiano Espresso & Wine Bar Exeter   @artigianoexeter

37. CHANDOS DELI

1 Roman Walk, Princesshay, Exeter, Devon, EX1 1GN.

You'll be spoilt for choice at the Exeter branch of this popular South West deli.

You'll find it in the city's modern Princesshay shopping area, so it's spacious and contemporary. And, as it's on the edge of the main walkway area by the city wall, you'll also find a relaxing spot to sit outside and enjoy some people watching.

After you've finished your espresso-based coffee from Bristol's Wogan Coffee, you really shouldn't leave without perusing the fabulous selection of gourmet delights from across the globe. Chandos is a deli in the proper sense of the word, and there are always lots of tempting items to buy including internationally jet-setting cheeses, antipasti, meats, wines and beers, alongside a good range from local producers.

The team has earned a reputation for its menu to eat in or take away, including pies, quiches, sausage rolls, baguettes and sandwiches (the latter created by an award winning sandwich designer). Keep a look out for special events like wine tasting evenings, too.

INSIDER'S TIP
TRY THE AWARD-WINNING SESAME CHICKEN SANDWICH WITH SPRING ONIONS AND CORIANDER

KEY ROASTER
Wogan

BREWING METHOD
Espresso

MACHINE
Rancillo

GRINDER
Mazzer

OPENING HOURS
Mon-Sat 9am-6pm
Sun 10am-4pm

www.chandosdeli.com   T: 01392 437379

f Chandos Deli Exeter   🐦 @chandosdeli

№38. DEVON COFFEE

88 Queen Street, Exeter, Devon, EX4 3RP.

evon Coffee has just celebrated its third birthday at its location in Exeter's Queen Street. The team still works to the motto of "good coffee, made well, by nice people" and is known for quality, friendly service and, of course, great coffee.

They now roast all their own coffee under the sister business Exe Coffee Roasters (XCR) and also retail freshly roasted coffee, both instore and online at www.execoffeeroasters.co.uk

New equipment this year includes a La Marzocco Linea PB machine and an EK43 grinder which are used in the making of a choice of espresso and several filter options from their own roasted coffee.

There's good coffee shop food available too, including cakes, pastries, toasties and butties – made with locally produced bread and fillings, wherever possible.

INSIDER'S TIP VISIT FOR ITS BARISTA AND ROASTING CLASSES

KEY ROASTER
XCR

BREWING METHODS
Espresso, V60, AeroPress

MACHINE
La Marzocco Linea PB

GRINDER
Mahlkonig EK43

OPENING HOURS
Mon-Sat 8am-6pm
Sun 10am-4pm

www.devoncoffee.co.uk   T: 07795 105250

f DevonCoffeeShop   🐦 @coffeedevon

MAP Nº 39. WILD THYME CAFE

5 Caen Field Shopping Centre, Braunton, Devon, EX33 1EE.

Wild Thyme Cafe is a central cog in Braunton's laid back beach culture and surf scene, and well known for serving speciality coffee, revitalising juices, smoothies, homemade cakes and great breakfasts. Safe to say the cafe is keeping hungry surfers, cyclists, holidaymakers and locals smiling.

Coffee and food is very important to the Johnston family who run Wild Thyme, a passion that stems from inspiration fired up by travelling the globe – with an added shot of a desire to serve a quality cup of the dark stuff. As a result, the cafe also hosts pop-up food events, with Indonesian, Thai and pizza nights regularly on the menu.

INSIDER'S TIP WILD THYME ALSO HAS AN EVENT CATERING SERVICE, WHICH INCLUDES A CRACKING HOG ROAST

All the baristas are trained by its coffee supplier, Origin, aiming for the highest standards possible. Complement your caffeine intake with one of the superb juices made with homegrown fruit and veg. The Performance Booster – a mash-up of beetroot, celery, carrot, apple and ginger - is the current big hit.

KEY ROASTER
Origin

BREWING METHODS
Espresso

MACHINE
Astoria

GRINDER
Mazzer Super Jolly Timer

OPENING HOURS
Mon-Sun 9am-4pm
Extended hours in the summer months

Gluten FREE

SOYA MILK AVAILABLE

WIFI

CYCLE FRIENDLY

OUTDOOR seating

FAMILY FRIENDLY

DISABLED ACCESS

www.wildthymecafe.co.uk　T: 01271 815191
f Wild Thyme Cafe　🐦 @wildthymecafe

40. HANNAHS SEALE-HAYNE

Howton Lane, Newton Abbot, Devon, TQ12 6NQ.

Hannahs Seale-Hayne isn't your usual speciality coffee venue. Housed in a striking Edwardian building on the outskirts of Newton Abbott, this cafe, bistro and for-good-cause venture offers internships to children and adults with disabilities, while serving Origin coffee and delicious seasonal food.

An emerging reputation for a great cup of coffee isn't the only thing growing at Hannahs – much of the fresh produce on its menu is grown onsite. All these fresh goodies are then transformed into a tempting range of Mediterranean dishes including salads, sandwiches and slow-cooked stews, so when the weather's good and you've grabbed a seat in the quad, you could easily be on the Spanish coast.

INSIDER'S TIP GRAB A COFFEE AND FRESHLY BAKED CAKE TO-GO FROM THE PANTRY, HANNAH'S LATEST EDITION

As much thought and care is taken over the espresso-based coffees as the food coming out of the kitchen, as the barista team makes sure that every cup is top quality. As they say at Hannahs, *'Life's too short for bad coffee.'*

KEY ROASTER
Origin

BREWING METHOD
Espresso

MACHINE
Sanremo

GRINDER
Sanremo

OPENING HOURS
Mon 8am-7pm
Tue-Sat 8am-10pm
Sun 9am-7pm

www.discoverhannahs.org   T: 01626 325800

f Discover Hannahs   🐦 @discoverhannahs

41. TANGERINE TREE CAFE

50 High Street, Totnes, Devon, TQ9 5SQ.

Bright orange chairs out front give the game away - yes, there's no missing the aptly named Tangerine Tree Cafe in characterful Totnes.

Famed for its indie shops, cafes and restaurants, you'll be in need of a stonking coffee once you've explored the whole of this pretty Devon town, and you'll find Tangerine Tree at the top end of the main street.

With two floors and tables out front, plus a peaceful walled garden, there are plenty of places to find a little nook. Wherever you choose to sit, you'll experience a warm welcome and a feel-good vibe which extends to the whole experience.

Owners Ness and Martin Turner are committed to a home-grown ethos, sourcing supplies locally and making the breakfast and lunch menus from scratch. Ness also whips up killer cakes, including dairy and sugar free options. There are loose leaf teas for non coffee drinkers and Luscombe juices from Devon, but it's the coffee that takes centre stage. The single origin is from the El Majahual region of El Salvador and purchased directly from the farmers by Clifton.

KEY ROASTER
Clifton

BREWING METHOD
Espresso

MACHINE
Cimbali

GRINDER
Mazzer Super Jolly

OPENING HOURS
Tues-Sat
8.30am-5pm

Gluten FREE

COFFEE BEANS AVAILABLE

SOYA MILK AVAILABLE

WIFI

OUTDOOR seating

FAMILY FRIENDLY

INSIDER'S TIP HIDE AWAY IN A COMFY LOUNGE CHAIR ON THE SECOND FLOOR

www.tangerinetree.co.uk   T: 01803 840853

f Tangerine Tree Cafe

42. BAYARDS COVE INN

27 Lower Street, Dartmouth, Devon, TQ6 9AN.

Modern artisan coffee meets medieval charm at this stone walled Tudor building – a former market house built in the 14th century.

Located in central Dartmouth with views out to the mouth of the River Dart, Bayards Cove Inn is a bustling daytime cafe as well as a restaurant and boutique hotel. The charming exterior offers a taste of the warm welcome you'll find from the team here, which is matched by the cosiness of its comfy leather sofas and – during the chilly months – a glowing wood burner.

Origin provides the coffee and also trains staff in how to get the best out of its beans – so you know you're in for a quality brew. Pair it with a lush homemade cake, a proper Devonshire tea of scones and cream (jam on top, natch), or stay for lunch and try one of the cafe's popular homemade burgers.

Four-legged friends are very welcome and well looked after, making this a perfect pit stop after one of the area's stunning coastal walks.

KEY ROASTER
Origin

BREWING METHOD
Espresso

MACHINE
Sanremo

GRINDER
Sanremo

OPENING HOURS
Mon-Sun
8am-10pm

INSIDER'S TIP FEELING ADVENTUROUS? ASK TO BORROW ONE OF THE PADDLE BOARDS ...

www.bayardscoveinn.co.uk   T: 01803 839278

f Bayards Cove Inn   🐦 @bayardscoveinn

43. COASTERS COFFEE COMPANY

Unit 1, Abbots Quay, Prince of Wales Road, Kingsbridge, Devon, TQ7 1DY.

A quiet corner of the South Hams is probably one of the last places you'd expect to find a booming speciality coffee trade, but thanks to Paul and Jackie from Coasters Coffee Company, the market town of Kingsbridge is being expertly caffeinated.

They use a changing guest espresso and filter coffee, often featuring local roasters Extract and Crankhouse and some from further afield such as Square Mile and Climpson & Sons. With a custom house blend from Clifton as the go-to cup and a range of beans and brewing equipment for sale, Coasters is a real find for the coffee enthusiast.

INSIDER'S TIP KEEP AN EYE ON COASTERS' FACEBOOK PAGE FOR NEWS ON FILTER TASTING AND CUPPING EVENTS

A fantastic selection of homemade sandwiches and panini, along with top notch cakes from Devon favourites, Peck & Strong and The Exploding Bakery, combine with homely touches such as comfy sofas, board games and a brimming bookcase, making this is a hub for everyone – not just the coffee connoisseur.

KEY ROASTER
Clifton

BREWING METHODS
Espresso,
Clever dripper,
V60, AeroPress

MACHINE
La Marzocco Linea

GRINDERS
Nuova Simonelli
Mythos One,
Malkonig K30 Vario,
Mazzer Super Jolly
x2, Baratza Preciso

OPENING HOURS
Mon-Fri
8.30am-6pm
Sat 8.30am-5pm
Sun 9am-2pm

T: 01548 853004

f Coasters Coffee Company @coasterscoffee

MAP Nº 44. BOSTON TEA PARTY

Jamaica House, 82-84 Vauxhall Street, Sutton Harbour, Plymouth, Devon, PL4 0EX.

BTP Plymouth is the newest member of the family-owned cafe group which are spread across the South West.

Based in Jamaica House on Sutton Harbour, like many of its siblings, it enjoys the grandeur of being in a historic building – this one Grade-II listed. The team has transformed the interior into two floors of cafe wonderland including a flower-enclosed outdoor seating area with stunning views over the marina towards the Barbican.

In true BTP style, it's characterful as a result of the use of an eclectic mix of upcycled, salvaged and restored furniture, as well as old gymnasium flooring on the walls and school chairs.

INSIDER'S TIP ÜBER FAMILY FRIENDLY, YOU'LL FIND BABY CHANGING, SPACE FOR PUSHCHAIRS AND TOYS AND BOOKS FOR LITTLE KIDS

Of course, it's the coffee and food you visit for, and everything is sustainably sourced, affordable and made inhouse. We especially like the breakfasts – including pancakes with bacon and maple syrup and eggs benedict, served with a good coffee (with locally sourced organic milk), from which you can choose from the medium or dark house roasts as well as guest filters.

KEY ROASTER
Extract

BREWING METHODS
Espresso, filter

MACHINES
La Marzocco
Linea for espresso,
Marco Jet for filter

GRINDER
Mazzer Major

OPENING HOURS
Mon-Wed
7am-9pm
Thurs-Sat
7am-11pm
Sun 8am-9pm

www.bostonteaparty.co.uk   T: 01752 267862

f Boston Tea Party Cafes   🐦 @btpcafes

Drinks
Gear
Knowledge

The Bristol based home of Sweetbird and Zuma has been supplying the coffee scene for over 18 years, and is a proud supporter of the South West Coffee Guide*

0117 953 3522

 @beyondthebean

*and know how to throw a mean launch party...

CORNWALL

Indy coffee venues

HUB ST IVES
MAP.№51 | PAGE.№97

MAP.№ 45. LIBERTY COFFEE

4 Northgate Street, Launceston, Cornwall, PL15 8BD.

Stalwart of the Cornish speciality coffee scene, Ben Statton of Liberty Coffee is on a mission. He's made it his personal cause to invigorate customers' tastebuds with the best speciality grade, single origin coffee he can get his hands on, sourced from a range of roasters including Origin, Clifton, Round Hill and Square Mile.

'We want to highlight how growing, sourcing, roasting and brewing speciality coffee differs from its commodity counterpart,' says Ben.

Located just around the corner from Launceston High Street, the cafe has undergone a revamp this year, but the commitment to brilliant coffee remains as strong as ever. A short and sweet coffee menu features espresso-based coffees along with black filter, which Ben reckons to be 'the true taster format.' There's also a must-try new cold brew which delivers a surprising array of flavour notes.

INSIDER'S TIP TRY A COLD BREW FOR A COMPLETELY DIFFERENT COFFEE EXPERIENCE

Equal care is taken over the real hot chocolate made from single origin cocoa, and seriously good cakes which are baked inhouse.

KEY ROASTER
Multiple

BREWING METHODS
Espresso, AeroPress, cold brew

MACHINE
La Marzocco Linea

GRINDERS
Mazzer Major Electronic x 2, Mahlkonig Vario, Nuova Simonelli Mythos One

OPENING HOURS
Mon-Sat
8.30am-5.30pm
Sun Open during summer months

www.liberty-coffee.co.uk   T: 01566 773223

f Liberty Coffee   🐦 @libcoffee

46. STRONG ADOLFO'S

Hawksfield, A39, Wadebridge, Cornwall, PL27 7LR.

There are loads of cafes that strive to push the boundaries but sadly fall short of the mark. Not so with Strong Adolfo's as it embodies the vision of owners John and Mathilda to a tee.

An effortless mix of Scandi cool, incredible food, speciality coffee and friendly vibe attracts an eclectic crowd of surfers, bikers, cyclists and foodies who've made this cafe a regular stop on their travels. Strong Adolfo's is not all smoke with no cigar though - in 2015 it was a finalist in *Food* magazine's Reader Awards in the South West's Best Cafe category.

Originally from Sweden, Mathilda has brought the Swedish tradition of fika (where everyone stops for a coffee break and something sweet) to the cafe, and there's a lovely selection of homemade cakes on offer including Swedish chocolate balls and a killer cloud cake.

In addition to coffee and cake, the breakfasts are famed - check out the homemade baked beans – as are scrummy seasonal dishes like wild mushrooms on sourdough, pulled lamb wraps and spicy falafel. In a world of mediocrity, we love its vision to be different. Make it a pit stop on your next trip along the Atlantic Highway - there's free parking and they love dogs too!

KEY ROASTER
Origin

BREWING METHODS
Espresso, Clever dripper, batch filter

MACHINE
La Marzocco

GRINDER
Simonelli

OPENING HOURS
Mon-Fri
8.30am-4.30pm
Sat 9am-5pm
Sun 9am-4.30pm

INSIDER'S TIP WATCH OUT FOR THE COOL EVENTS AND SUBCULTURAL HAPPENINGS

 Gluten FREE

 SOYA MILK AVAILABLE

 WIFI

 CYCLE FRIENDLY

 OUTDOOR seating

 FAMILY FRIENDLY

 DISABLED ACCESS

www.strongadolfos.com   T: 01208 816949

f Strong Adolfo's   🐦 @strongadolfos

MAP 47. 108 COFFEE HOUSE

108c Kenwyn Street, Truro, Cornwall, TR1 3DJ.

Getting a quality coffee on the way to work can be hard enough, let alone getting your hands on a good cup once you're *in* the office, but 108 Coffee has answered the Truro workforce's caffeine woes, offering an artisan coffee delivery service for the masses.

By text, email or phone, the city's busy workers can have a carefully crafted Origin coffee from one of 108's highly skilled baristas transported to their door for free. The cafe delivers home made breakfasts and lunches too, working to keep any under-desk rumbling tums at bay.

INSIDER'S TIP GRAB A SLICE OF BANANA BREAD IF YOU CAN - IT'S THE LOCALS' FAVE

This popular city centre coffee shop isn't just for commuting coffee lovers however, as the cosy cafe is a great spot in which to relax and spend a little time – there are comfy chairs in which to while away the hours with a good book and a great selection of homemade bakes to tempt the sweet-toothed visitor.

KEY ROASTER
Origin

BREWING METHODS
Espresso, V60

MACHINE
La Marzocco
Strada MP 3 group

GRINDERS
Mazzer Robur,
Mahlkonig
Tanzania

OPENING HOURS
Mon-Fri 7am-6pm
Sat 8am-6pm

www.108coffee.co.uk   T: 07582 339636

f 108 Coffee House   @108_coffee

MAP № 48. GOOD VIBES CAFE

28 Killigrew Street, Falmouth, Cornwall, TR11 3PN.

If you were to describe the vibe at Good Vibes Cafe, then "good" would certainly cut it – but it also wouldn't really tell the whole story. You'd have to add qualities like simple, wholesome and authentic to paint the full picture of this funky cafe in Falmouth.

Herbivores and health nuts will love it here – more than half the menu is vegan or vegetarian, featuring the likes of homegrown organic heirloom tomatoes and spiced halloumi in colourful Middle Eastern flat bread salads, hot chocolate with coconut, and smoothies packed with avocado, peanut butter and banana.

INSIDER'S TIP TRY GOOD VIBES' UNIQUE MATCHA GREEN TEA LATTE WITH BONSOY

And then, of course, there's the coffee. Since they opened shop in 2013, owners John and Hannah Hersey have pared back the coffee offering to a tried-and-true Origin blend so they can, *'focus on getting one thing right – all the time,'* says John. It's certainly working as the quality is top notch.

With upcycled furniture, cool artwork and that relaxed atmosphere, it's a place to escape the crowds of summer holiday makers and enjoy the good, simple things in life.

KEY ROASTER
Origin

BREWING METHOD
Espresso

MACHINE
La Marzocco
Linea 3 group

GRINDER
Malkonig K30 x 2

OPENING HOURS
Mon-Sat
8.30am-5.30pm
Sun 10am-2pm

T: 01326 211870

f Good Vibes Cafe 🐦 @tgood_vibes_cafe

^{MAP No.}49. PICNIC CORNWALL

14 Church Street, Falmouth, Cornwall, TR11 3DR.

Opening only two years ago, the multi-award winning Picnic Cornwall has already become something of an institution in arty Falmouth. Recognised for its quality coffee offering, it has a stream of regular customers, many of whom make a daily pilgrimage for an Origin brew.

And rightly so, as the small, well-trained barista team sets its standards high. The commitment to coffee looks to evolve even further with plans to launch a new food van to spread a little Picnic coffee and deli magic further afield.

Its new owner, Jo Forman, fell in love with Cornwall and moved to the county after a career in technology, so it's no surprise that one of her aims is for Picnic to encourage visitors to explore the surrounding landscape. Ask your barista for the local lowdown if you're new in town. Jo's continuing to build on Picnic's ethos of quality and local sourcing and every item in the deli comes from Cornwall. She has big plans to extend the Picnic family further by opening another coffee shop and deli, so watch this space.

KEY ROASTER
Origin

BREWING METHOD
Espresso

MACHINE
La Marzocco FB80

GRINDER
Mazzer Luigi

OPENING HOURS
Mon- Sun
8.30am-5.30pm with extended hours in summer

INSIDER'S TIP PICNIC DOES GREAT HAMPERS AND WILL EVEN DELIVER ONE TO YOU ON THE BEACH

www.picniccornwall.co.uk   T: 01326 211655

f Picnic Cornwall   🐦 @picniccornwall

50. GYLLY BEACH CAFE

On Gyllyngvase Beach, Cliff Road, Falmouth, Cornwall, TR11 4PA.

It's hard to beat the setting of this coffee shop and cafe. Right on Gyllyngvase beach, beneath Pendennis Castle in Falmouth, Gylly Beach Cafe is loved by a host of regulars, from uni students to dog walkers, families, swimmers – and even knitting and bowls groups. 'It's all about soul, spirit and smiles,' says manager Mark Agnew.

The cafe has been in the same family since 2000 and many members of staff have long associations with owners Simon and Viv Daw and their cafe, such is the popularity of the place. But a major redesign and refurbishment in 2008 saw Gylly come into its own, with wall to ceiling windows opening it up, bringing the outdoors in – whatever the weather.

They're hot on sustainability too and thought goes into everything – from sourcing food to recycling and energy use – and this dedication has earned them a gold star award from the Green Tourism Business Scheme. In addition, 'Everything is homemade wherever possible' says Mark, 'or sourced in Cornwall'.

Needless to say, as much care goes into the coffee, and the team makes full use of the expertise and ongoing training from Cornwall's Origin roastery.

KEY ROASTER
Origin

BREWING METHOD
Espresso

MACHINE
La Marzocco

GRINDER
Espresso Italiano

OPENING HOURS
Mon-Sun
9am til late

INSIDER'S TIP ONE OF THE BEST SUNDAY NIGHT MUSIC VENUES IN THE COUNTY

www.gyllybeach.com   T: 01326 312884
f Gylly Beach Cafe   @gyllybeachcafe

£51. HUB ST IVES

4 Wharf Road, St Ives, Cornwall, TR26 1LF.

Everyday favourites are taken to new levels at Hub. This cool little spot on the picturesque St Ives waterfront takes inspiration from American comfort food: nachos served with slow-smoked pulled pork, 28-day-aged rare breed Cornish beef burgers and local craft beers.

Naturally, its approach to coffee is equally discerning, so don't expect your average cup of Joe. Espresso based drinks and filtered coffees come care of the house seasonal blend from Origin, while rotating guest roasts are sourced from local artisan roasters such as Extract.

Great for groups and family get-togethers, the Hub is spread out over two levels, both of which offer expansive views over the water. Of an evening, stop by for a cocktail and live music, or simply watch the world go by from the balcony seating.

INSIDER'S TIP BUZZING IN SUMMER, VISIT DURING THE OFF SEASON FOR A CHIN WAG WITH THE RESIDENT COFFEE GEEKS

You can start the day here too, of course; the pared back breakfast menu is served until 11.30am, and includes bacon and fluffy pancakes with proper maple syrup - plus plenty of good coffee to get you revved up and ready to go.

KEY ROASTER
Origin

BREWING METHODS
Espresso, filter

MACHINE
La Marzocco Strada

GRINDER
Nuovo Simonelli Mythos One

OPENING HOURS
Mon-Sun
Summer
7am til late
Winter
9am til late

www.hub-stives.co.uk T: 01736 799099

f hub.stives 🐦 @hubstives

MAP Nº 52. THE YELLOW CANARY CAFE

12 Fore Street, St Ives, Cornwall, TR26 1AB.

The Yellow Canary Cafe is firmly ingrained in the history of St Ives, with three generations of the Haase family having worked tirelessly to uphold the fine reputation of this family run coffee shop.

Although it was first established in 1972, the cafe has rolled with the times, keeping up with trends and ensuring its standards are of the highest quality. The cafe has developed a devoted local following as a result of delicacies such as homemade biscotti and the fine speciality coffee.

If you want to track it down, it's hard to miss, even tucked away as it is down cobbled Fore Street, due to its vibrant yellow sign, gently swaying in the sea breeze.

In addition to the superb coffee, supplied by local Cornish roaster Origin, owner Paul has worked hard on the menu and is thoroughly committed to using the best local ingredients and suppliers. *'We pride ourselves on sourcing all our food within a 10 mile radius, especially the cakes – they're from just round the corner,'* he smiles.

KEY ROASTER
Origin

BREWING METHODS
Espresso,
AeroPress

MACHINE
La Marzocco

GRINDER
Mazzer Major E

OPENING HOURS
7 days a week
March - November
Summer
7am-10pm
Winter
9am-5pm

INSIDER'S TIP GET A VOUCHER FOR A FREE COFFEE ON THE YELLOW CANARY WEBSITE

www.theyellowcanary.com   T: 01736 797118

f The Yellow Canary Cafe   🐦 @yellowcanarycaf

53. THE BREW HOUSE

Harbour Head, Porthleven, Cornwall, TR13 9JA.

With all the excitement of its Shoreditch store opening this year, it's easy to overlook Origin's original cafe – but a visit to The Brew House in Porthleven will make you fall in love all over again. And if you've yet to experience the roaster's cool little Cornish hangout, then you're in for a treat.

INSIDER'S TIP
TRY A COLD BREW PUNCH – IT TASTES LIKE A NEAPOLITAN ICE CREAM

Set in the heart of the traditional fishing village on the south coast, it's minimally furnished with natural wood seating and tables, echoing the surrounding Cornish landscape. Perch on a stool at the window and gaze out over the water while indulging in one of Origin's special edition coffees or new espresso blends, Resolute and Pathfinder. You'll be sampling single estate beans that are roasted down the road at Origin HQ and include micro-lot coffees that have been sourced exclusively for The Brew House on Origin's direct trade trips.

Naturally, there's a wide variety of brew methods to choose from here, and a team of highly skilled baristas who, living and breathing coffee, are ready to share the love. The food offering matches the quality of the coffee, so there's plenty of reasons to visit this very cool Cornish coffee venue.

KEY ROASTER
Origin

BREWING METHODS
Espresso, V60, AeroPress, Chemex, Alto Air, cold brew

MACHINE
Custom La Marzocco Strada 2 EP

GRINDERS
Nouva Simonelli Mythos One x 2, Mahlkonig EK43

OPENING HOURS
Mon-Sun 9am-5pm
Open Easter to October half term and December 20-January 3

www.origincoffee.co.uk/the-brew-house   T: 01326 574337

f The Brew House Porthleven   @thebrewhouse1

MOBILE

Indy coffee venues

IVAN'S COFFEE

MAP.№56 | PAGE.№103

MAP N° 54. TINCAN COFFEE CO

Major music festivals and events across the South West and UK.

Tincan Coffee Co and its fleet of super cool 1960s and 70s vintage trucks is now rolling into its sixth year of serving up quality speciality coffee to festival revellers, sports fans and event goers across the South West.

INSIDER'S TIP KEEP 'EM PEELED FOR TINCAN COFFEE CO TRUCKS ON BBC1 AND SKY1 THIS YEAR

This year alone has seen the chaps crafting fine coffee (with regular guest single origins) across a huge number of festivals including Shambala, Festival No 6, Secret Garden Party, Forgotten Fields and Goodwood Revival. The trucks also continue to revive the hungry, delivering award winning cakes, artisan toasties and revitalising smoothies.

'I've been in the coffee industry for 20 years and proud to be an independent business trading at some of the highest profile festivals and events,' says owner Adam White. 'We're the sole specialist coffee provider at The Queen's Club tennis, for example, and we like to think we're still the "#BestCoffeeInAnyField,"' he continues.

Tincan is going from strength to strength and while its signature trucks remain iconic, Adam is also tinkering with plans for his first bricks and mortar venture which should open in Bristol by 2016.

KEY ROASTER
Clifton

BREWING METHODS
Espresso,
bulk brew drip

MACHINES
La Spaziale S5

GRINDERS
Mazzers

OPENING HOURS
Open as long as the
event is open

www.tincanevents.com   T: 07725 880581

f Tincan Events   🐦 @tincanevents

№55. READS ROASTBOX

Limekiln Farm, Sherborne, Dorset, DT9 6PS and at events across the South West.

In 2001 Giles Dick-Read took a trip to collect his first roaster which he transported back home in a horsebox.

Whether or not that sparked an idea for a mobile coffee van is a question you'll have to ask him, but what we can say is that, since spring last year, a horsebox has taken a star role in the Reads Coffee operation. *'It seemed entirely appropriate that when we started a mobile cafe it should be in a converted trailer,'* says Giles, who heads the family run roastery near Sherborne.

Now, at regular events around Dorset, Somerset and beyond, Reads Roastbox – formerly known as The Little Grey Cafe - has become synonymous with the delivery of speciality coffee and gluten-free goodies.

It's a mini coffee factory really, but so simply designed that it's easily adapted to suit festivals and events as a breakfast bar, retail outlet, espresso bar and even a mobile microroastery-come-training-unit. *'We can demo espresso blends, teach and even roast from it,'* says Giles. *'It's tremendously satisfying to be collecting green coffee one day, roasting the next and making drinks in the middle of a field another day. If I could just grow it too, we'd be a complete operation!'*

INSIDER'S TIP FORGET DOG AND CHILD FRIENDLY, THIS IS HORSE FRIENDLY

KEY ROASTER
Reads

BREWING METHODS
Espresso,
drip, pourover

MACHINE
Gaggia

GRINDERS
Gaggia, Bunn

OPENING HOURS
Available
on request

---

www.readscoffee.co.uk   T: 01935 481010

f Reads Coffee Roasters   🐦 @reads_coffee

56. IVAN'S COFFEE

At events and festivals across the South West.

Former drummer and roadie Ivan Bunyard had his fair share of bad coffee while travelling on the road with musicians such as Paloma Faith and Mumford and Sons, so he came up with his own solution.

Enter stage right Ivan's Coffee, a 1962 Volkswagen Splitscreen van, owned for 12 years and lovingly restored by Ivan and his wife Deby. The cool little mobile coffee shop has since been all over the place, supplying speciality coffee to festival goers and surfers at the beach. Ivan, who's based in mid Devon, uses coffee from local roasters Crediton Coffee and Crankhouse Coffee with milk from Ashclyst Farm Dairy – you'll also find some guest coffee surprises too. Expect a relaxed, outdoorsy coffee experience with a few good tales to accompany it.

As a new venture this autumn, Ivan will be teaming up with The Bike Shop in Tiverton to offer a brew bar, espresso based drinks and locally made cakes. They'll be using a Rocket Evoluzione Giotto and a Sanremo Sr. 70 Evo grinder. We suggest getting on your bike hitting the road right now.

KEY ROASTERS
Crankhouse Coffee, Crediton Coffee

BREWING METHODS
Espresso, drip filter, cold brew

MACHINE
Fracino retro lever with dual fuel

GRINDER
Fracino C3r

OPENING HOURS
On request

INSIDER'S TIP ASK NICELY AND IVAN MIGHT LET YOU SIT IN THE VAN TO DRINK YOUR BREW

www.ivans-coffee.com   T: 07796 128057

f Ivans Coffee   @ivanscoffee

MORE GOOD CUPS

So many cool places to drink coffee ...

MAP 57. THE SCANDINAVIAN COFFEE POD
62 St George's Place, Cheltenham, GL50 3PN.
www.scandinaviancoffeepod.com
T: 01242 633701
f The Scandinavian Coffee Pod   @podcoffee

MAP 58. THE ROOKERY
35 Marlborough Street, Faringdon, SN7 7JL.
www.therookery.me.uk
T: 01367 242030
f The Rookery - Beautiful Things   @therookeryoxon

MAP 59. THE GREEN BIRD CAFE
11 Margaret's Buildings, Bath, BA1 2LP.
www.greenbirdcafe.co.uk
T: 01225 487846
f The Green Bird Cafe   @greenbirdcafe

MAP 60. PICNIC COFFEE
5 Burton Street, Bath, BA1 1BN.
www.picniccoffee.co.uk
T: 01225 789700
f Picnic Coffee on Burton   @picnic_bath

MAP 61. BOSTON TEA PARTY
19 Kingsmead Square, Bath, BA1 2AE.
www.bostonteaparty.co.uk
T: 01225 314826
f Boston Tea Party Cafes   @btpcafes

MAP 62. THE GREEN ROCKET CAFE
1 Pierrepont Street, Bath, BA1 1LB.
www.thegreenrocket.co.uk
T: 01225 420084
f The Green Rocket Cafe   @greenrocketcafe

MAP 63. JIKA JIKA
4 Brunel Square, Bath, BA1 1SX.
www.jikajika.co.uk
T: 01225 469253
f Jika Jika   @jika_jika

MAP 64. BAKERS AND CO.
193 Gloucester Road, Bristol, BS7 8BG.
www.bakersbristol.co.uk
f Bakers and Co Bristol   @bakersandco

65. CAFE RONAK

169 Gloucester Road, Bristol, BS7 8BE.

www.caferonak.co.uk

T: 01173 070392

f Cafe Ronak 🐦 @caferonak

66. THE BRISTOLIAN CAFE

2 Picton Street, Montpelier, Bristol, BS6 5QA.

www.thebristolian.co.uk

T: 01179 192808

f The Bristolian Cafe 🐦 @bristoliancafe

67. NO 12 EASTON

12 High Street, Easton, Bristol, BS5 6DL.

www.12easton.com

f No12 Easton 🐦 @no12easton

68. FRISKA

70 Queen's Road, Bristol, BS8 1QU.
(and Victoria Street)

www.friskafood.com

T: 01179 300989

f Friska 🐦 @friskafood

69. BEATROOT CAFE

20-21 Lower Park Row, Bristol, BS1 5BN.

www.beatrootcafe.co.uk

T: 01173 763714

f Beatroot Cafe 🐦 @beatrootcafe

70. FULL COURT PRESS

59 Broad Street, Bristol, BS1 2EJ.

www.fcpcoffee.com

T: 07794 808552

f Full Court Press – Speciality Coffee 🐦 @fcpcoffee

71. SPICER+COLE

1 Queen Square Avenue, Bristol, BS1 4JA.

www.spicerandcole.co.uk

T: 01179 220513

f Spicer and Cole 🐦 @spicerandcole

72. BRIGSTOW LOUNGE

Millennium Promenade, Bristol, BS1 5SY.

www.brigstowlounge.co.uk

T: 01173 250898

f Brigstow Lounge 🐦 @brigstowlounge

73. THE RIVER HOUSE

7 The Bridge, Frome, Somerset, BA11 1AR.

www.riverhousefrome.co.uk

T: 01373 464847

f The River House 🐦 @riverhousefrome

74. CROCKER & WOODS

27 Catherine Hill, Frome, Somerset, BA11 1BY.

www.crockerandwoods.com

T: 07773 766009

f Crocker & Woods 🐦 @crockerwoods

75. THE DANCING GOAT

31 Parr Street, Poole, Dorset, BH14 0JX.

www.thedancinggoat.co.uk

T: 07973 642466

f The Dancing Goat 🐦 @thedancinggoat1

76. NUMBER 35 COFFEE HOUSE AND KITCHEN

35 High West Street, Dorchester, DT1 1UP.

www.coffeehouseandkitchen.com

T: 01305 549269

f Number 35 Coffee House & Kitchen 🐦 @no35coffeehouse

77. BROOM WAGON COFFEE

3 Cross Street, Seaton, Devon, EX12 2LH.

www.cafebroomwagon.com

T: 07747 105918

f Broom Wagon Coffee 🐦 @cafebroomwagon

MAP 78. BOSTON TEA PARTY

Monkton House, 53 High Street, Honiton, Devon, EX14 1PW.

www.bostonteaparty.co.uk

T: 01404 548739

f Boston Tea Party Cafes 🐦 @btpcafes

MAP 79. BOSTON TEA PARTY

21 Tuly Street, Barnstaple, Devon, EX31 1DH.

www.bostonteaparty.co.uk

T: 01271 329070

f Boston Tea Party Cafes 🐦 @btpcafes

MAP 80. BEATSWORKIN COFFEE N SKATE

9 Queens House, Barnstaple, Devon, EX32 8HJ.

www.beatsworkin.net

T: 01271 321111

f Beatsworkin Coffee n Skate 🐦 @beatsworkinuk

MAP 81. THE BIKE SHED CAFE

Barnstaple Square, Barnstaple, EX32 8LS.

www.bikesheduk.com

T: 01271 328628

f The Bike Shed, Barnstaple 🐦 @bikesheddevon

MAP 82. CREDITON COFFEE COMPANY

1 Market Square House, Market Street, Crediton, Devon, EX17 2BN.

www.creditoncoffee.co.uk

T: 01363 775065

f Crediton Coffee Company 🐦 @creditoncoffee

MAP 83. BOSTON TEA PARTY

84 Queen Street, Exeter, Devon, EX4 3RP.

www.bostonteaparty.co.uk

T: 01392 201181

f Boston Tea Party Cafes 🐦 @btpcafes

MAP 84. CAFE AT 36

36 Cowick Street, Exeter, Devon, EX4 1AW.

www.cafeat36.co.uk

T: 01392 410352

f Cafe at 36 🐦 @cafeat36

MAP 85. JACKA BAKERY

38 Southside Street, The Barbican, Plymouth, PL1 2LE.

T: 01752 291265

f Jacka Bakery 🐦 @jackabakery

MAP 86. TUBESTATION

Trebetherick Hill, Polzeath, Cornwall, PL27 6TB.

www.tubestation.org

T: 01208 869200

f Tubestation Polzeath 🐦 @tubestationcrew

MAP 87. RELISH FOOD AND DRINK

Foundry Court, Wadebridge, Cornwall, PL27 7QN.

www.relishcornwall.co.uk

T: 01208 814214

f Relish Food & Drink 🐦 @relishcornwall

MAP 88. WOODS CAFE

Cardinham Woods, Bodmin, Cornwall, PL30 4AL.

www.woodscafecornwall.co.uk

T: 01208 78111

f Woods Cafe 🐦 @woodscafekernow

MAP 89. ESPRESSINI

39 Killigrew Street, Falmouth, Cornwall, TR11 3PW.

www.espressini.co.uk

f Espressini 🐦 @espressini39

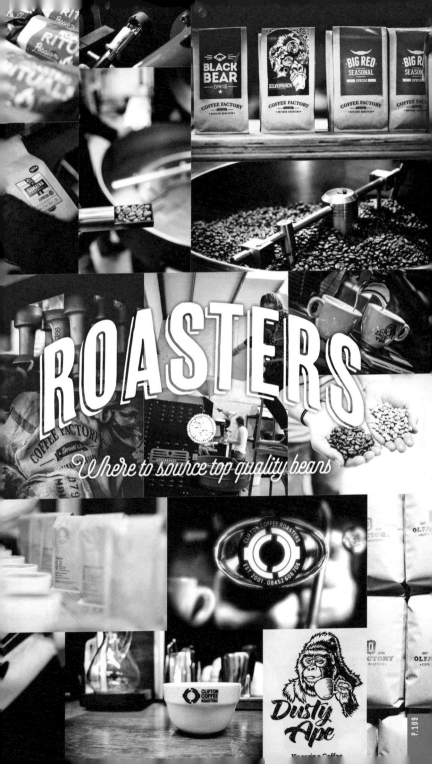

ROASTERS

Where to source top quality beans

90. RAVE COFFEE

Unit 7, Stirling Works, Love Lane, Cirencester, Gloucestershire, GL7 1YG.

www.ravecoffee.co.uk   T: 01285 651884

f RAVE Coffee   🐦 @ravecoffee

Great ventures usually begin with bold ideas and a bucketful of passion, and Vikki and Rob Hodge from RAVE Coffee clearly have this potent mix in abundance.

In 2009, the couple emigrated to Australia, with the aim of escaping the corporate world. Days before departure they had a light-bulb moment and decided to try something totally different down under - and the RAVE Coffee van was born.

'FIRE HER UP AND SHE ROARS LIKE A VULCAN BOMBER WHILE PRODUCING A DELICIOUS ASSAULT ON THE NASAL PASSAGES'

Throughout their Antipodean adventure they had the chance to work with some of the best baristas and roasters in Sydney before returning to the UK in 2011, to open their own roastery.

The business has spread like wildfire, leading to a bigger roasting site and in-house cafe in Cirencester, and it's now a vibrant, international company employing a team of coffee-mad employees - all drawn to RAVE by the same enthusiasm for a great brew.

Right now the team is committed to investing in cutting edge technology to protect the environment. The guys have installed a shiny new Loring coffee roaster sourced from California, which complements the quality of green coffee perfectly - producing a clean cup with greater control, and reducing energy consumption and emissions by 80 per cent. *'Fire her up and she roars like a Vulcan Bomber while producing a delicious assault on the nasal passages. You'll smell us for miles when we're roasting,'* Rob beams like a proud father.

RAVE roasts and supplies single origin coffee and its own blends across the globe to cafes, coffee chains, five star airports and retail customers. And now its first international roastery and cafe is set to open in Alberta, Canada. Headed up by another member of the Hodge coffee clan, Dean Smolicz, it's well worth a visit (if you're ever in Canada!) with an epic view of the Rockies.

COFFEE BEANS AVAILABLE
SOLD ON SITE **& ONLINE**

COFFEE COURSES AVAILABLE

MAP № 91. CLIFTON COFFEE ROASTERS

C2, Island Trade Park, Bristow Broadway, Avonmouth, Bristol, BS11 9FB.
www.cliftoncoffee.co.uk   T: 08452 606706

f Clifton Coffee Roasters 🐦 @cliftoncoffee

One of the leading roasters in the South West, Clifton Coffee Roasters has been at the forefront of the region's speciality coffee movement for over 15 years.

Its remit is wide, and in addition to supplying the wholesale industry with high quality speciality coffee, its expertise extends to the supply and maintenance of espresso and filter brewing equipment. It also delivers bespoke education programs to meet a wide variety of barista client needs, so they are well equipped to make the best coffee possible.

COFFEE BEANS AVAILABLE · SOLD ON SITE · **& ONLINE**

Sourcing green coffee direct from producers, as well as European specialist importers, Head of Coffee Andrew Tucker was recently in El Salvador during the harvest, where he set up a direct trade relationship with a producer in Santa Ana. Buying coffee from a single estate called Finca Bella Vista, its E1 Project is a European exclusive to Clifton Coffee Roasters.

The range is constantly expanding to include seasonal espresso blends alongside rotating single origin offerings available as both filter and espresso profiles. Andrew and the roast team utilise Diedrich CR-25 and IR-12 roasters, as well an IR-1 and a Joper Barrel for sample roasting.

'BUYING COFFEE FROM A SINGLE ESTATE CALLED FINCA BELLA VISTA, ITS E1 PROJECT IS A EUROPEAN EXCLUSIVE'

Holding weekly cuppings every Friday morning with customers, the team continues to provide a unique 24/7, 365 day engineering service to an expanding range of wholesale customers.

Home coffee brewers are also well catered for with an expansive online shop displaying many items for making delicious coffee at home.

MAP №92. TWODAY COFFEE ROASTERS

135-137 St Michaels Hill, Bristol, BS2 8BS. | 26 Union Street, Bristol, BS1 2DP.
www.twodaycoffee.co.uk   T: 01179 299191
🐦 @twodaycoffee

There are few things that can return us grown-up folk to that kid-in-a-sweet-shop kind of excitement, but with the smell of newly roasted coffee thick in the air, a wall lined with different varieties of beans and a set of scales waiting to be filled, Twoday Coffee Roasters can certainly take any coffee fiend back in time.

Born out of 15 years of travel and inspired by Tokyo coffee culture, Frank and Petra Deane created this Bristol-based roastery and shop to supply locals with fresh beans. Nine years later and the customers still can't get enough.

COFFEE BEANS AVAILABLE SOLD ON SITE & ONLINE

The clue to its success is in the name, as the couple strive to deliver speciality coffee to their loyal customers within two days of it being roasted. It's actually not such a difficult task as Twoday usually sells out half way through the second day.

'THE SMELL OF NEWLY ROASTED COFFEE IN THE AIR, A WALL LINED WITH DIFFERENT VARIETIES OF BEANS AND A SET OF SCALES WAITING TO BE FILLED'

With a couple of shops in the city and a dedicated roastery, the budding-barista can source everything they need from Frank and Petra to satiate the coffee cravings. And that includes brewing equipment, coffee cups, friendly advice and a pick and mix of freshly roasted beans, of course.

MAP Nº 93. WOGAN COFFEE

2 Clement Street, Bristol, BS2 9EQ.
www.wogancoffee.co.uk   T: 01179 553564

f Wogan Coffee - Bristol 🐦 @wogancoffee

With more than 45 years' experience, Wogan Coffee enjoys the privileged position of being the longest established and largest independent coffee roaster in the South West. It's been sourcing and importing the world's finest green beans, then roasting and crafting them to create outstanding bespoke coffee in Bristol since 1970.

'CUSTOMERS CAN SAMPLE SOME OF THE SPECIALITY COFFEE FOR FREE ON FILTER FRIDAYS'

Very much a family affair, the roastery is run by Adrian Wogan who nurses the coffee through the process with an infectious passion. *'We're proud to have some of the most respected palates, baristas and espresso machine technicians in the country,'* he says. *'And we draw on our wealth of knowledge to deliver the best. We're also proud to have full control over the whole process, from sourcing to roasting to training, and enjoy long-standing relationships with over 40 farms.'*

Wogan Coffee goes that little bit further too, to help the communities where its coffee is grown. *'La Bastilla, Nicaragua, is one of our single estate, direct trade farms, with which*

our close involvement has led to educational opportunities for the local children,' says Adrian. *'Some of our team recently visited the farm to present degree certificates to a number of our sponsored students, of whom we are incredibly proud. On our latest visit, we secured two new exciting micro-lot processing types – honeyed and natural - both exclusive to us.'*

At the heart of the operation is a classic 1968 90kg Probat roaster and a smaller, 30kg roaster, used in a supporting role for small batch roasts as well as "coffee of the month" offers – different, highly prized, speciality grade, single origin beans, sourced, cupped and roasted to enhance their very best characteristics.

It's recently opened a new training and cupping room, used daily for barista training, brew courses and tasting sessions which everyone is welcome to join. There's also a new trade counter where customers can sample some of the speciality coffee for free on Filter Fridays.

COFFEE BEANS AVAILABLE
SOLD ON SITE
& ONLINE

COFFEE COURSES AVAILABLE

№94. EXTRACT COFFEE ROASTERS

Unit 1, Gatton Road, Bristol, BS2 9SH.

www.extractcoffee.co.uk   T: 01179 554976

f Extract Coffee Roasters 🐦 @extractcoffee

Extract Coffee Roasters began life as a family business with one simple aim - to produce and serve great coffee. Since its early days, selling home-roasted coffee from a cart on Bristol's iconic College Green, it's come a long way to become one of the UK's leading coffee companies.

Following the restoration of Betty, a vintage Probat roaster from 1955, and establishing a permanent premises in Bristol, Extract is now not only a production facility, but also a destination hub for the coffee community.

Collaborations with other local producers have made for exciting projects, including a couple of coffee IPAs – and plenty of caffeine fuelled parties. The roastery itself has hosted supper clubs, barista BBQs, a film screening and the launch of last year's *Indy Coffee Guide*, as well as a monthly barista workshop for the burgeoning home market.

Aside from roasting and serving good coffee, Extract is also working to close the gap between farmer and consumer. This year saw head roaster David Faulkner fly out to Kenya to begin the latest exciting collaboration.

'There was great coffee on offer at the Chania Estate in Kenya, he says. *'But what was most interesting was how the coffee was processed. I'd love our next mission to explore this influence on the coffee. We'll be looking to spend more time at source in the near future, working with the farmers to trial new processing methods.'*

'COLLABORATIONS WITH OTHER LOCAL PRODUCERS HAVE MADE FOR EXCITING PROJECTS, INCLUDING A COUPLE OF COFFEE IPAS'

A return to Chania Estate is booked for the harvest later this year. With new projects on the horizon, Probat Betty's family is growing too, including new restoration projects in the pipeline for a 120kg Probat and 30kg Petroncini. Exciting times ahead.

COFFEE BEANS AVAILABLE SOLD ON SITE **& ONLINE**

COFFEE COURSES AVAILABLE

95. LITTLE & LONG

Unit 50, Station Road Workshops, Station Road, Bristol, BS15 4PJ.
www.littleandlong.com   T: 07956 638669

f Little and Long Coffee Roasters 🐦 @littleandlongcc

Little & Long's founder, Saskia Falconer's deep passion for coffee was sparked by growing up in coffee-mad New Zealand, as well as her experience of working with two different coffee roasters in Italy.

COFFEE BEANS AVAILABLE SOLD ON SITE **& ONLINE**

It was in Italy in particular that she gained the valuable expertise needed to set up Little & Long in Bristol: *'I roasted with two very un-Italian roasters who, instead of over-roasting beans had a philosophy that centred around selecting great beans, roasting them gently and letting the natural flavours of the beans be the star of the show. At the time this definitely wasn't the usual approach in Italy!'*, she comments.

As a result, her motto when roasting coffee now is, *'watch, listen, be patient, think a little, and be rewarded!'* which has led to the set up of a full blown roastery in Bristol, with Saskia's pride and joy, an old Probat roaster, at the centre of the action.

The beans are roasted in small batches, with Saskia keeping a constant eye on the key numbers so that the coffee reaches the optimum roasting point. This approach has led to a loyal following for her product. *'Good coffee shouldn't be the exception, it should be the norm,'* she says.

In the last 12 months, Little & Long has worked closely with several customers to develop individual blends for their cafes. *'Creating blends is a great part of the job, playing around with flavour combinations to get the perfect cup profile is very satisfying,'* says Saskia.

'WATCH, LISTEN, BE PATIENT, THINK A LITTLE, AND BE REWARDED!'

MAP N° 96. ROASTED RITUALS COFFEE

Unit 18, Kenn Court, Roman Farm Road, Bristol, BS4 1UL.
www.roastedritualscoffee.com   T: 01172 440098

f Roasted Rituals Coffee 🐦 @roastedrituals

Dropping anchor in Bristol seemed like the right thing to do in 2013 when Patrick and Tahi Grant-Sturgis were looking for the right mix of community spirit and big city coffee cravings.

With a collective background in commercial coffee roasting, along with farming and agricultural experience, they set up Roasted Rituals with a desire to make speciality coffee both approachable and affordable.

Joined in 2014 by head roaster, Courtney Taylor Jackson (previously of renowned Seven Seeds in Melbourne), a common ground was quickly established and trading begun.

With quality the driving force, the team uses modern roasting techniques and over 30 years of collective barista experience, to deliver coffee with distinctive flavour and consistency.

'ADVICE IS FREELY GIVEN ON HOW BEST TO BREW YOUR FRESH BAG OF COFFEE WHILE YOU SIP YOUR FLAT WHITE'

Of course, quality doesn't happen by chance, so cupping every roast keeps the team's palates' sharp.

And in addition to delivering quality beans, all wholesale customers receive free on and off site barista training along with regular roastery visits to keep the flame of passion burning strong. An ever changing array of retail coffee is available through the website as well. And with freshness a priority, expect snappy service.

Alternatively, you could pay a visit to the vintage Citroën coffee van on Bristol's Blackboy Hill, where advice is freely given on how best to brew your fresh bag of coffee while you sip a flat white.

Taking advantage of Tahi's extensive food background, the team has recently set up Tradewind Espresso on Whiteladies Road. *We feel like the cafe culture in Bristol has real potential, and are super excited to bring a little of the experiences we gained down under to the green capital of Europe,'* says Tahi. If you're in Bristol we highly recommend you pop in for a brew. It looks like exciting times lie ahead for the Roasted Rituals team.

COFFEE BEANS AVAILABLE
SOLD ON SITE
& ONLINE

MAP No 97. DUSTY APE

Bath Beverages Ltd, Marsh Farm Roastery, Hilperton, Wiltshire, BA14 7PJ.
www.dustyape.com   T: 01225 753838

f Dusty Ape 🐦 @dustyape

COFFEE BEANS AVAILABLE SOLD ON SITE **& ONLINE**

Dusty Ape Coffee, co-founded by good friends Phil Buckley and Evan Metz, roasts exceptional single estates and blends from its Wiltshire roastery.

The two self-confessed 'coffee nuts' first met at their sons' football match, discovering they shared a burning passion for the dark cup. Their aim is simple: to turn people on to quality, speciality coffee - and away from bucket-loads of coffee-flavoured milk at high street chains.

Dusty Ape is making headway with a growing demand for its carefully crafted coffees – sales more than doubled in the past 12 months. This growth has led to an exciting new investment: meet "Kong" Dusty Ape's new 12kg Probat roaster, which has allowed them to up the ante and treble production.

It's not just about the roasting, of course, with the guys priding themselves on meticulous sourcing of the highest grade arabica beans and holding daily cupping rituals to ensure the highest consistency with the right balance of flavours.

'MEET "KONG" DUSTY APE'S NEW 12KG PROBAT ROASTER'

In order to help make great coffee accessible to a wider audience (without being overly prescriptive about how it should be drunk), Phil and Evan are running Knowing Coffee appreciation and training courses, to allow people to experience the bean to cup process first hand. The sessions cover bean sourcing, roasting, cupping and brewing – exploring a wide variety of coffee making methods like espresso, pourover and cold brew. *As people's tastes evolve and their coffee knowledge deepens, we provide advice, skills and equipment to help them explore all its possibilities,'* says Evan. *'Caffeine may provide a short term hit but coffee knowledge stimulates a lifetime journey for people.'*

№ 98. ROUND HILL ROASTERY

Unit 14, Midsomer Enterprise Park, Wheelers Hill, Midsomer Norton, Somerset, BA3 2BB.
www.roundhillroastery.com   T: 01761 435888

f Round Hill Roastery   🐦 @roundhillcoffee

The founder of Round Hill Roastery, Eddie Twitchett, may be young, having set up the roastery when he was just 23, but what he lacks in years at the grind (excuse the pun), he certainly makes up for in passion, excitement and commitment to quality coffee.

Much of Eddie's inspiration comes from the renowned Colonna & Small's in Bath, where Eddie was a regular customer and a fan of what award winning barista and owner, Maxwell Colonna-Dashwood, was doing. Eddie convinced Maxwell to give him some training, leading Eddie to enrol at the London School of Coffee.

For Eddie it's about the world of flavours and the desire to share this excitement, while giving customers the best experience possible. *It's the interaction I love, the conversations about flavour that keep me obsessed.*

COFFEE BEANS AVAILABLE
SOLD ON SITE **& ONLINE**

COFFEE COURSES AVAILABLE

I enjoy talking to customers - whether they're wholesale clients or people passing by at a farmers' market.'

'SPECIALIST COFFEE SHOPS ARE ASKING FOR A DIFFERENT COFFEE EVERY WEEK DUE TO THE DEMAND FOR OUR FLAVOURS'

In the last 12 months, things have really moved on – in 2015 Round Hill roasted 25 tonnes of coffee, 30% more than in 2014, and by the time you read this Eddie and his burgeoning team will be in much bigger premises, allowing for further expansion. *Things have been crazy,'* he explains, *'the interest and demand for our coffee has really grown, especially with our single farm, single co-operative, no blended coffee ethos. Specialist coffee shops such as Full Court Press in Bristol are asking for a different coffee every week due to the demand for our flavours.'*

ROUND HILL ROASTERY

MAP № 99. READS COFFEE

Limekiln Farm, Thornford Road, Sherborne, Dorset, DT9 6PS.

www.readscoffee.co.uk   T: 01935 481010

f Reads Coffee Roasters   🐦 @reads_coffee

Despite educating the man who went on to crack Enigma, it remains a secret to many that Sherborne has been home to a busy coffee roastery for ten years.

Giles Dick-Read has been roasting on the edge of town since 2005. *'I've been fascinated with espresso machines, in fact machines of any kind, for as long as I can remember, and I've been working with coffee since I was in Vancouver and the Pacific North West for six months in 1993.'*

'I STARTED ROASTING TO TEACH MYSELF ABOUT THIS APPARENT DARK ART OF SMOKE AND MIRRORS'

On return to the UK, Giles took a Solo cup and drink-through lid to Sinclair Beecham at Pret A Manger. *'He'd never seen one! A role within the organisation was born overnight and I found myself running the coffee operation. It seems ages ago and the coffee world has moved on a great deal, but back then this was the cutting edge - The First Wave, perhaps.'*

The move into roasting was inevitable. *'I started roasting in 2001 on a 15kg Ambex, as much as anything to teach myself about this apparent dark art of smoke and mirrors'*. That saw the business through to early 2014, when Reads took delivery of the first Probat

25/2 in the UK. *'I love it, roasting the beans, sourcing coffee, the whole lot – I even still collect green coffee myself whenever possible. I'm an advocate for roasting single origins, the more interesting, the better – although time has taught me significant lessons about how to create espresso blends with a broad appeal. In short, I roast coffee I like, the way I like to drink it.'*

Coupled with that is an absolute desire to help customers brew coffee at its best. *'I started out training, and remain a trainer - be it teaching newcomers how to use an espresso machine in a cafe, or home experts how to get the best out of a stovetop, it's all an essential part of the coffee process. Roasting, after all, just produces the ingredient – people need to learn what to do with it to taste it at its best.'*

A family affair, Reads runs from the converted dairy at Limekiln Farm, a few hundred metres south of Sherborne. Open days are planned during 2016 with the Reads Roastbox Cafe being joined by other interesting mobile food operations for, *'an eccentric corral, to which this place is perfectly suited,'* says Giles.

COFFEE BEANS AVAILABLE

SOLD ON SITE & ONLINE

COFFEE COURSES AVAILABLE

100. BRAZIER COFFEE ROASTERS

Unit 5, Nightingale Farm Units, West Hatch, Somerset, TA3 5RH.
www.braziercoffeeroasters.co.uk   T: 01823 353317

f Brazier Coffee Roasters 🐦 @brazierroasters

Claire and Tom Brazier came up with the idea of starting their own coffee roasting business over a particularly good cup of coffee in Brisbane.

Originally from the city, Claire worked there as a barista for many years, before the pair decided to take their love of coffee to Somerset – a world away from sub-tropical Australia.

'WE SOURCE ONLY SPECIALITY COFFEE, FOCUSING ON HIGHEST-ALTITUDE PRODUCERS'

Even after landing in Somerset they spent the next few years making return trips to Australia, researching and training with some of the country's best artisan roasters. Only then did they take the plunge and drive from England to Holland, where they loaded their 6kg Giesen W6 roaster on to a trailer to drive it home again and establish Brazier Coffee Roasters. This was in the winter of 2015 and that same trailer has since become a mobile coffee house serving Brazier brews.

'We get our green beans from a variety of small independent importers who work closely with farmers at origin,' says Claire.

Brazier specialises in high-altitude coffee and one of Claire and Tom's favourite single origins at the moment is a washed and sundried Bourbon and Typica from Burundi in land-locked east Africa, grown at 1950 metres above sea level.

'We source only speciality coffee, focusing on highest-altitude producers,' says Tom, adding, *'you can really taste the difference. We have three signature blends, Altitude, Seasonal and Filter, and we always have some great single origins.'*

The pair also have plans to travel to Indonesia to visit coffee farms and establish some direct trade links.

Espresso machines, barista gear, machine servicing and coffee training are all also supplied at the Brazier roastery in the tiny Somerset village of West Hatch on the outskirts of Taunton, and Tom and Claire host cupping events at cafes to encourage customers to try brewing their coffee at home, too.

COFFEE BEANS AVAILABLE SOLD ON SITE **& ONLINE**

COFFEE COURSES AVAILABLE

MAP № 101. AMID GIANTS & IDOLS

59 Silver Street, Lyme Regis, Dorset, DT7 3HR.
www.amidgiantsandidols.com   T: 07928 790254

f Amid Giants & Idols   🐦 @amidgiantsidols

On talking to Amid Giants and Idols' founder, Xanne Carey, what jumps out most powerfully is her passionate commitment to creating the very best coffee she possibly can. Within the first year of business, Xanne reached the semi finals of the 2013 UK Barista Championships, and says, *'we've dedicated our every waking moment to learning about coffee'*. She's the real deal.

'THE ROASTERY'S PRIDE AND JOY IS A LOVINGLY RESTORED 80 YEAR OLD ROASTER CALLED OTTO'

Amid Giants and Idols is a micro-roastery in stunning Lyme Regis, carefully sourcing some of the most fabulous, flavoursome green coffees, roasting them with great care to ensure maximum aroma, flavour profiles and freshness. By seasonally selecting beans from a wide variety of farms, Xanne can ensure there is both flavour and freshness in every cup.

The roastery's pride and joy, a lovingly restored 80 year old roaster called Otto, takes centre stage, and combined with 21st century technology and Xanne's honed skills, Otto produces a consistent result.

The company works on the premise of no fuss and no pretension, as she explains, *'we focus on combining the best coffee, equipment, training and passion, to provide a truly special coffee experience.'* And if recent coverage in titles such as *Caffeine* is anything to go by, it looks like they're nailing it.

COFFEE BEANS AVAILABLE
SOLD ON SITE & ONLINE

COFFEE COURSES AVAILABLE

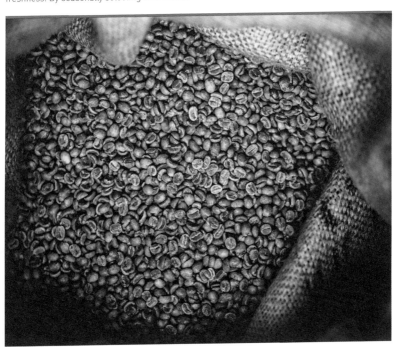

102. COFFEE FACTORY

Samurai Buildings, Seaton Junction, Axminster, Devon, EX13 7PW.
www.coffeefactory.co.uk   T: 01297 551259
f Coffee Factory   🐦 @coffee_factory

offee Factory's Danny Parfitt has a strong chef background and it's his culinary skills that have given him the perfect foundation on which to produce top quality coffee. He's now been in speciality coffee for over a decade – both as a barista competing in the UK Barista Championships, and as a roaster since 2007.

The Coffee Factory is really gathering pace and its reputation continues to flourish in the speciality coffee world: it's recently moved to a much larger unit, and invested in a vintage 22kg 1950s Probat UG22 roaster, lovingly restored with all the latest mod cons, *'we mashed her up and mixed in some modern tech,'* says Danny. They've had this roaster on their wish list for a long time so are understandably over the moon, naming her Dorothy Vadar (Danny's a *Star Wars* fan).

'WE MASHED HER UP AND MIXED IN SOME MODERN TECH,' SAYS DANNY

As well as giving Dorothy the mother of all make-overs, they've opened an on-site cafe,

Factory Cafe, where you can sample the blends and watch the magic happen.

Coffee Factory continues to produce its popular seasonal flagship blends such as Black Bear, a classic Brazil blend with a malty, chocolate, easy drinking taste, and Big Red with a fruitier, sharper taste – a perfect guest coffee, Danny suggests. Two or three single origins are also always available, refreshed every three to six weeks to ensure the highest quality.

Joining forces with Bean & Ground Coffee Club, Coffee Factory is also growing its coffee and gift subscription services, and is looking to open a fully functioning training room where coffee fans can attend coffee courses.

Before then, you can buy your beans online or pop into the roastery and cafe and say hello to Dorothy!

COFFEE BEANS AVAILABLE
SOLD ON SITE
& ONLINE

MAP.№ **103.** CRANKHOUSE COFFEE

35 Masterson Street, Exeter, EX2 5GR.
www.crankhousecoffee.co.uk   T: 07588 020288

f Crankhouse Coffee 🐦 @crankhouseroast

A lot's happened at Crankhouse since last year's guide was published and its owner and roastmeister Dave Stanton's been cranking things up a gear.

Inexorably linked to the cycling world, the Devon based roaster has launched two new coffees suited to the racing calendar in its Spring Classic and Grand Tour blends and has been represented at the Tour of Britain on the Madison Genesis team bus.

Dave's also supported local barista and good friend Jesse Dodkins at this year's UKBC finals in Glasgow. *'He was using Crankhouse Coffee and I was so proud to have it up there on the judges' table, having been prepared by such a talented barista,'* says Dave.

Of course, there have been challenges too - not least in the selecting of green beans for roasting, and Dave says, *'there's an increasing number of importers with offer lists that are getting longer and longer, so sorting the good from the not-so-good is time consuming. I'm also relying on only one palate (i.e. mine) which isn't ideal. Luckily I've had input from a number of people who work in coffee around Exeter and we've created a little Cupper Club. Getting input from these folk on a regular basis has been invaluable - and it's been fun.'*

These cupping sessions have also developed into public cupping and tasting classes in addition to the barista training and support Dave offers his wholesale customers. Crankhouse fans can also get involved through the online store which offers retail coffees, brewing equipment and has a news blog about what's going on, *'and I'll be extending things with brew guides and more equipment as time goes on,'* he says.

COFFEE BEANS AVAILABLE
SOLD ON SITE & ONLINE

COFFEE COURSES AVAILABLE

'WE'VE CREATED A LITTLE CUPPER CLUB AND GETTING INPUT FROM THESE FOLK ON A REGULAR BASIS HAS BEEN INVALUABLE'

MAP Nº 104. VOYAGER COFFEE ROASTERS

Unit 6, Mardle Way Business Park, Buckfastleigh, TQ11 0JL.
www.voyager.coffee   T: 01364 644440
f Voyager Coffee Roasters **🐦** @voyagercoffee

'**W**ith more than 15 years experience and over 300 customers across the South West, the recently re-branded Voyager Coffee uniquely boasts two state of the art Genio roasters, which are fired up daily by Master Roaster, Rachael Jowitt, and the bubbly Lou.

'Having a mainly female cast of roasters, you won't find any handlebar moustaches here, but you will find great coffee, hand roasted in small batches with the greatest attention to detail,' Rachael says. 'It's the only way to draw the best and most interesting flavours from unique coffees. We focus on getting great flavours and making sure our customers have the comfort of consistency.'

'However, the real fun is in cupping and refining the roasting process,' she continues, 'we love to gather the team for cupping every week to share opinions - it's at the heart of everything we do.'

Voyager produces a Globetrotter Series of single origin specialities and some outstanding espresso blends, including Kaldi's Odyssey, which holds the only Taste of the West gold awarded to a coffee in 2015, as well as the very popular blend of triple certified organic beans, Fatroc.

Considering that Andrew Tucker, founder of Voyager started his working life on an Antarctic research station and has travelled through most continents, it's no surprise that Voyager is a roaster with an international perspective. 'I've always loved great coffee and travelling, so putting the two together is a dream come true!' he says.

'THE REAL FUN IS IN CUPPING AND REFINING OUR ROASTING – IT'S AT THE HEART OF EVERYTHING WE DO'

Voyager Coffee also runs a wide range of barista courses and is a Sanremo espresso machine specialist, helping coffee businesses across the South West benefit from its full range of market leading coffee equipment.

105. OLFACTORY COFFEE ROASTERS

MP.N°

The Old Brewery Yard, Lower Treluswell, Penryn, Cornwall, TR10 9AT.
www.olfactorycoffee. co.uk   T: 01326 259980

f Olfactory Coffee Roasters 🐦 @olfactorycoffee

It's not everyone who manages to find their calling in life, but here's a case of someone who did.

Angel Parushev was all set for a career in law, which is where he'd be now if he hadn't taken a part time barista job when he was at university. His natural talent and understanding of coffee became evident and after perfecting his barista skills, Angel made the move into roasting.

'I WANT TO GIVE VISITORS THE CHANCE TO LEARN ABOUT THE PROCESS OF ROASTING, AND GIVE THEM AN INSIGHT INTO THE WORKMANSHIP '

And just a year (of some experimentation) after hitting on the idea of setting up a roastery, Olfactory was born.

Set in a 200-year-old former brewery building on the outskirts of Penryn, Olfactory aims to, *release the very best flavours; striving to do justice to every step of the process before it reaches us, and as we roast it for our clients,* explains Angel.

With a wealth of knowledge, research and skill, Angel and his team roast coffee with profiles that bring the best sweetness, flavour and richness out of each coffee bean that passes through the door. *We have a very high tech roaster, so we can profile the roast and experiment with it so that the resulting coffee is the best it can be.*

Preferring to keep contact with, and buy direct from the farmers, as well as working closely with highly trusted green bean brokers, Angel puts ethics high on the agenda. His business is mostly wholesale, but an open door policy means you can pop in for a chat anytime. *I want to give visitors the chance to learn about the process of roasting and give them an insight into the workmanship that goes into creating our product. That way Olfactory's clients are empowered to make excellent coffee everyday.*

COFFEE BEANS AVAILABLE
SOLD ON SITE

COFFEE COURSES AVAILABLE

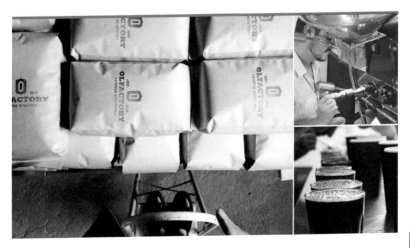

MAP Nº 106. ORIGIN COFFEE

The Roastery, Wheal Vrose Business Park, Helston, Cornwall, TR13 0FG.
www.origincoffee.co.uk   T: 01326 574337

f Origin Coffee Roasters 🐦 @origincoffee

There have been some exciting developments for the Origin Coffee team since last year's guide was published.

The big one was the opening of a London outpost in Shoreditch which both showcases Origin coffees and also includes a brew bar, signature drinks and an education centre.

Education and training is a key part of Origin's work – it offers barista education and training at both its Cornwall and London centres, through the Speciality Coffee Association of Europe's Diploma System, as well as home brewing courses. You know you're in expert hands too as the team has gathered an impressive number of awards this year; in the

'RECENT TRIPS TO EL SALVADOR, NICARAGUA AND COLOMBIA HAVE BROUGHT MORE INCREDIBLE COFFEES BACK HOME'

UK Barista Championships, Origin's William Pitts came ninth and its head of wholesale, Dan Fellows, came fourth, placing him top barista in Cornwall along with the Best Newcomer accolade.

Origin holds fast to its position as a leading speciality coffee roasters with founder and owner Tom Sobey at the helm and ensuring that relationships at source are key to the business. Recent trips to El Salvador, Nicaragua and Colombia have developed strong partnerships with farmers and brought more incredible coffees back home. One of its special edition coffees is a release of the highly acclaimed Esmeralda Boquete Geisha, the world's most acclaimed varietal from one of the most impressive farms growing it.

New look packaging has taken Origin back to black and seen the return of its illustrations, and kit-wise there's now a second Loring Smart Roast, sitting alongside the original one in the roastery, enabling some post blending options.

Check out the new espresso blends, Resolute Espresso and Pathfinder Espresso too, which show Origin goes from strength to strength when it comes to producing delicious flavour profiles.

COFFEE BEANS AVAILABLE
SOLD ON SITE & ONLINE

COFFEE COURSES AVAILABLE

107. COFFEE TRAINING AND CONSULTANCY BY COFFEA ARABICA

Leaze Farm, Leaze Lane, Blagdon, Somerset, BS40 7XH.
www.coffeaarabica.co.uk　T: 07766 533157

f Daisy Rollo Coffea Arabica　🐦 @daisyrollo

Just as a sommelier or oenologist likes to get right to the essence of a good wine and to trace the vintage back to its roots, so Daisy Rollo wants to get to the very essence of speciality coffee and discover its origins and spend time in the countries where it's grown.

After these trips, Daisy brings back her experiences and knowledge, integrating it into her work as a coffee trainer and consultant. Her company, Coffea Arabica, was launched over a decade ago and since 2008 has been centred around her Leaze Farm Coffee School near Bristol.

Daisy, who hails from Cancale in Brittany, developed her interest in food and wine working for Michelin starred restaurants in France and the UK.

Drawing on experience working with The London School of Coffee and Union Hand Roasted, her school offers a range of professional courses from basic and intermediate barista training to latte art, brewing and team management workshops.

Every aspect of producing a cup of coffee is important, but for Daisy the key that lies at the heart of the whole process is the link with the producers, which is why she makes her annual pilgrimages, seeking out the growers and farmers in speciality coffee growing regions.

Recent trips include visits to Costa Rica, India, Panama, Ethiopia, Vietnam and Cuba. 'Travelling to the plantations and meeting the people is my passion. It gives me a great platform from which to teach and share information with baristas,' she says. 'Some people in the coffee world like to do competitions, to work at becoming the best, but I've invested my time in a different way. For me it's all about showcasing the people at origin, that's what really fascinates me.'

BREW
GLOSSARY

STRUGGLING TO KEEP UP WITH THE LATEST BREW METHODS AND TERMINOLOGY? Q GRADER JAMIE TREBY EXPLAINS THE LINGO ...

'There are basically two main methods of brewing,' says Jamie, *'immersion brewers and pourover/drip methods. Understanding which ones you like and which brew methods are similar should help you make a choice in cafes and at home.'*

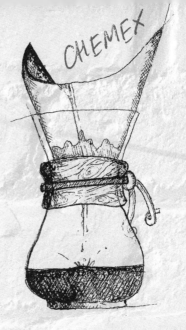

CHEMEX

AEROPRESS

A syringe-shaped filter brew method that includes an element of mechanical extraction with the water being forced through the coffee and filter paper.

ALTO AIR

An open-sided conical brewer, adaptable to many filter papers such as V60, Melitta or Kalita.

CAFETIERE

Also known as the french press. A coarse metal filter is plunged through coffee grounds which are immersed in water. High on body with characteristic residue in the bottom of the cup afterwards.

CHEMEX

A classic jug/filter combination invented in the fifties, the Chemex is both brew method and serving jug in one. It has circular or square filter papers characterised by the method of folding, leaving three sheets on one side and one on the other.

CLEVER DRIPPER

Essentially a Melitta cone with a fancy bottom plate, you can brew with full immersion until you place the brewer on your cup or jug, then lift the bottom plate and allow the brewed coffee to drain out.

COLD BREW

Coffee brewed cold as opposed to brewed hot and then chilled, either through an immersion method or a tower, where the water drips slowly through the coffee bed.

DRIP/BATCH BREWERS

Very similar in principle to pourovers, and more likely found in high volume cafes. They have a showerhead instead of one stream of water and varying degrees of automation. Some will use paper filters and others fine mesh. The key thing with bulk brewing, though, is to always check on the hold time, because the coffee can quickly lose its volatile compounds (they give it that wonderful smell) leaving a baked or metallic flavour note.

EK SHOTS/COFFEE SHOTS

Originating from a Barista Championships performance, the EK refers to Mahlkonig's EK43 grinder which has taken the cafe world by storm. Essentially a lungo (long shot of espresso) made on the espresso machine but giving a considerably better cup of coffee than the lungo which was often characterised by over-extracted bitterness.

ESPRESSO

Given that cappuccinos, lattes, and a whole host of cafe drinks start as an espresso, this is an important brew method. However, espresso is subject to perhaps the widest variation of any style out there. Modern baristas will happily discuss brew ratios: the dry weight of the coffee 'in' to the wet weight of the liquid 'out' and use this to control quality. Traditionalists may still quote in terms of weight and time and volume of shot, so ask the barista – they should be able to talk about whatever method they choose.

KALITA

A manufacturer of pourover filters, generally referring to the 'wave', which are conical in shape with sinuating sides and flat bottomed filter papers.

MELITTA

Another cone shaped filter method, with the differentiation here being a pinched draining point at the bottom of the cone rather than a point.

POUROVER

Manual brewing characterised by having a flow of fresh water through the bed of coffee, so you get a quicker, more aggressive extraction particularly around the outside of the ground coffee particle. Grind size must be spot on to get the best result.

SYPHON

This heats the water in an enclosed chamber using the resulting pressure to force the water into contact with the coffee in an upper chamber. When the heat's removed, the subsequent cooling then draws the coffee through a cloth filter back into the bottom chamber which is used to serve the coffee.

V60

Manufactured by Hario of Japan, this is the classic conical shaped brewer. It can be plastic, glass or ceramic, and all use the conical filter papers.

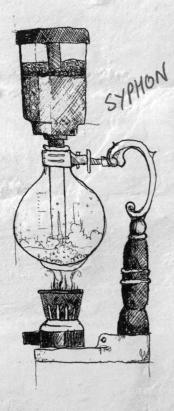

SYPHON

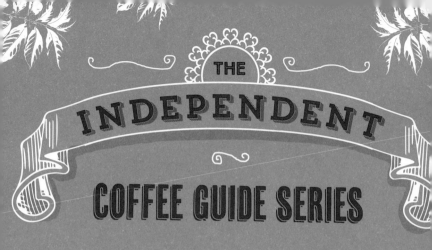

MEET THE COMMITTEE

IT TAKES PASSION, ENTHUSIASM, BLOOD, SWEAT AND TEARS TO CREATE A DEDICATED GUIDE TO THE BEST COFFEE IN A REGION – AND HAPPILY, THE INDY COFFEE GUIDE'S SOUTH WEST COMMITTEE WERE UP FOR THE CHALLENGE AGAIN

MAXWELL COLONNA-DASHWOOD

Maxwell is the three time UK Barista Champion and three time World Finalist who is always keen to get behind the bar at Colonna & Small's to brew and serve coffee. He's just started Colonna Roastery, focusing on sourcing and roasting the rarest high scoring coffees, and recently published *Water For Coffee*, a manual for the industry and enthusiast on the science of water and its affect on the flavour of coffee. He's also National Co-ordinator of the SCAE UK Chapter and sits on the World Barista Development Committee.

ED GOODING

Ed is the UK and Ireland sales manager for Bunn, which supplies coffee equipment across the globe. Ed says, *'I'm fortunate to work in an industry that I love - and at a very exciting time. We are watching quality become the norm, which is fantastic. Oh, and I also enjoy wearing Lycra and drinking wine'.*

ANDREW TUCKER

Head of Coffee for Clifton Coffee Roasters, Andrew is a SCAA qualified lead instructor and has spent over 13 years in hospitality and catering. *'I've focused on speciality coffee while working across Canada, Australasia, France and the UK - in a variety of retail and wholesale roles,'* he says, *'at Clifton I oversee the green coffee procurement and roasting, as well as managing our wholesale and education programme.'*

NICK COOPER

Nick is a founding director of Salt Media, the South West marketing company and publishing house that hand crafts **food** magazine, *The Trencherman's Guide* and the *Indy Coffee Guides*. You'll mostly find him drinking coffee – recently at the best coffee shops in the north of England in the creation of the *Northern Indy Coffee Guide*, and also in Glasgow and Edinburgh for the Scottish guide which launches in January 2016.

Meet
YEO VALLEY

ONE OF THE BIGGEST SUPPORTERS OF THE INDY COFFEE
GUIDE IS THE SOMERSET-BASED AND FAMILY RUN,
ORGANIC DAIRY FARM

The largest family-owned dairy business in the UK, Yeo Valley is a major success story for the South West, and it's been owned and run by the same family for more than 50 years.

'We've been farming in the beautiful Yeo Valley since 1961, since my parents bought the farm here in Blagdon,' says Tim Mead. Now it covers 1,200 acres of farmland and has 420 award winning British friesian cows.

The team prides itself on putting in the extra effort to look after its land and livestock, as well as supporting other British family farms. 'It's at the heart of everything we do,' says Tim. 'All our milk is supplied through the South West based Organic Milk Suppliers Cooperative (OMSCo). And by working together we're able to help lots of smaller family farms keep going, and we think that's the right way to farm.'

Yeo Valley holds dear to its principle of farming smaller herds, too: 'it means happier, healthier cows,' he says, 'so our dairy herd is split in to two separate farms.

'We operate a rotational farming model which means that not only do we grow grass for our cows to eat, we grow our own cereals too. By growing our own crops and looking after our soil, we can ensure that only great food goes into our cows, ensuring that only great milk comes out.'

Yeo Valley not only produces a range of milk and dairy products, you can also visit its organic garden and tea room or its YVHQ Canteen which showcases seasonal organic produce with a fantastic view of the Yeo Valley. And don't forget to finish with a coffee made from British roasted organic fair trade beans.

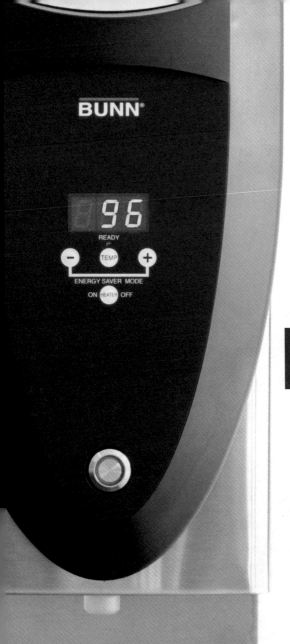

H3EA

HOT WATER DISPENSER

PRECISION
TEMPERATURE
CONTROL
CONTEMPORARY
DESIGN

BUNN.COM

INDEX